Happy New Year —

Salgia ~
Enjoy this book —
Maybe a few tips and
several laughs will find
its way to you.
Always remember —
You Belong To
Somebody ☺!

All my love —
Mommy

RUSSELL
RULES

RUSSELL RULES

11 LESSONS ON LEADERSHIP FROM THE TWENTIETH CENTURY'S GREATEST WINNER

Bill Russell

with David Falkner

DUTTON

DUTTON
Published by the Penguin Group
Penguin Putnam Inc., 375 Hudson Street, New York, New York 10014, U.S.A.
Penguin Books Ltd, 27 Wrights Lane, London W8 5TZ, England
Penguin Books Australia Ltd, Ringwood, Victoria, Australia
Penguin Books Canada Ltd, 10 Alcorn Avenue, Toronto, Ontario, Canada M4V 3B2
Penguin Books (N.Z.) Ltd, 182–190 Wairau Road, Auckland 10, New Zealand

Penguin Books Ltd, Registered Offices: Harmondsworth, Middlesex, England

Published by Dutton, a member of Penguin Putnam Inc.

First Printing, May, 2001
1   3   5   7   9   10   8   6   4   2

LIBRARY OF CONGRESS CATALOGING-IN-PUBLICATION DATA
Russell, Bill.
Russell rules : 11 lessons on leadership from the twentieth century's
greatest winner / Bill Russell with David Falkner.
p.   cm.
ISBN 0-525-94598-9 (alk. paper)
1. Russell, Bill, 1934–   2. Basketball players—United States—
Biography.   3. Boston Celtics (Basketball team)
4. Leadership.   I. Falkner, David.   II. Title.
GV884.R86 A3 2001
796.323'092—dc21
[B]   2001025331

Printed in the United States of America
Set in Goudy
Designed by Eve L. Kirch

*This book is dedicated to my family and friends.
Most especially, my friend Wilt;
my daughter, Karen; my father; and my best friend, Marilyn Nault*

CONTENTS

CONTENTS

Foreword

By Bill Bradley

O F ALL THE PLAYERS WHO EVER PLAYED THE GAME OF BAS-
ketball, Bill Russell is the first player that I would pick
to start a team. He is the greatest winner in basketball history—
eleven NBA championships in thirteen years. Some players
can amass individual statistics. Only one has had the strength
and focus to keep his team a champion for over a decade. And
team victory is the essence of basketball. In the 1961–62 season, Wilt Chamberlain averaged fifty points per game, but Bill
Russell won the MVP.

A great team is like a five-pointed star; each game, another
player can be the reason for victory. That's the way it was with
the Boston Celtics of Russell's era. He was surrounded by a talented group of teammates, but the team somehow belonged to
him. In the end, Red Auerbach officially recognized his leadership by selecting him as the player-coach of the Celtics. In that
role, without an assistant, he proceeded to win yet another two
championships.

To achieve Russell's level of success requires not only
physical ability, but also strength of mind and spirit. Only his

teammates knew the level of his intensity. They saw him throw up before most games. They saw him play with injury. They heard him in the huddles. They felt his competitive fire. They witnessed him thinking through the game before he even stepped foot on the court. They saw him do whatever was needed to win, game in and game out.

Russell always knew what he was doing on the court. A great winner is, above all, self-aware. He understands the impact that he has on other players. For example, one of Russell's great strengths was shot-blocking. He would jump straight up, timing his leap with the jump of his opponent, extend his arm and push the ball toward a teammate in its first foot of arc; or he would swoop in from behind, avoiding body contact with his opponent, and sometimes without the opponent's awareness, block the shot seemingly from out of nowhere. After that happened to a player several times, he could never be sure that he had a safe shot if Russell was within ten feet of him, which meant that he often threw himself off by changing his shot in anticipation of a Russell block. Tom Meschery, one of the few NBA alumni who is a poet, once wrote a poem about Russell. He entitled it "Eagle with a Beard." Many an NBA lay-up was missed because players feared the eagle with a beard was swooping down on them.

In 1997, I wrote a book entitled *Values of the Game*, which focused on ten values I had learned from basketball, such as discipline, selflessness, resilience, perspective, and courage. I was surprised when the book became the number-two best-seller on the business book list. Then I realized that those traits that typify a successful team also characterize successful organizations in general. That's why observations about basketball and life, coming from a perennial champion like Russell, have something to say to other organizations that want to win each year. A man who transformed a team into a dynasty knows about motivation, sacrifice, and teamwork as well as the best CEOs.

In forty-five years of public life, Bill Russell's dignity has never been diminished—his integrity remains intact. His answers are never hedged, usually original, and always honest. He knows friendship is deeper than slight, and as his teammates can confirm, once you are his friend you have been given a glorious gift. The cackle of his laugh epitomizes his joy of living. His record as basketball's greatest winner will stand for many years, perhaps forever, but the attractive thing about Bill Russell is how he has worn his accomplishments. That, even more than his achievements, makes him worthy of our admiration.

He certainly has mine.

Eleven rings, eleven lessons in winning

I PLAYED BASKETBALL FOR TWENTY-ONE YEARS. THE TEAMS I played for won championships eighteen times in those years. From the day I began as a junior varsity player at Mc-Clymond's High School in Oakland to my last day as player-coach of the Boston Celtics in 1969, winning was not only a habit but also a way of life for me. I learned from it, used it, incorporated it into my way of seeing the world. I haven't played a formal game of basketball since 1969. I've never wanted to. From time to time people ask me why. My answer is always the same: I didn't want to be Bill Russell of the Boston Celtics because I would have had to get myself to a certain level again, and unless I could be at that level, I wouldn't accept anything less.

When I played, I really didn't pay that much attention to what people wrote about me. I didn't close my eyes exactly—I was always aware of what went on around me—but I mainly kept my own counsel because what I did was never for anyone else's approval. All I was ever interested in was to do what I did as best I could. Period. The payoff was in using my skills, the most comprehensive skills in the game at that time, to the fullest and winning more championships that anyone else in team sports.

But the past became the present when, in August 1998, some close friends expressed their concern that, as the century was coming to a close and folks began looking retrospectively at the greatest this or the greatest that of the century, my name and that of my team would be discussed. We would inevitably be included in the written profiles of famous people, extraordinary moments, and celebrated accomplishments. It struck me that if anyone could effectively tell my story, it would be me. This was my chance to share with generations who may have only seen the Boston Celtics in black-and-white footage on cable television what team winning was all about. I was enticed to make the difficult transition from being William F. Russell of Mercer Island, Washington, to being Bill Russell, Boston Celtic, and sports legend. Being fundamentally private, William F. Russell is the person I am most comfortable being, but Bill Russell is the persona who millions listen to, and I felt I had a story to tell. That story is of the power of winning as a team, the impact of not only outplaying your opponents, but outthinking them and of reaching levels of success that all people can get to if they understand their strengths, their limitations, and the roles they are called upon to play.

It began in May 1999, when *Sports Illustrated* named the Boston Celtics as the "greatest team of the twentieth century" and me as "the greatest team player in history." *Sports Illustrated* wasn't alone. HBO recognized me as "the greatest winner of all time," and in the prior month *USA Today* featured former UCLA basketball coach John Wooden in their long legend series where he graciously called me "the most important college player and pro player of all time." John is one of the great coaches and inspirational leaders of any century.

Over the last couple of years I have resumed my interest in public speaking and have been speaking regularly to corporations across America, large and small, on translating the essence of "Celtic Pride" to their corporate cultures and customer relationships. In all those presentations, there hasn't been one where a CEO, senior sales exec, or the host of the meeting hasn't come up to me afterward to say, in effect, "Bill, we couldn't write fast enough. Why not share your lessons in leadership and winning in a format where it becomes a versatile and practical reference for everyone." Those requests have clearly served as a catalyst for me to think about a book.

However, an even more powerful prompting came from my friend Wilt Chamberlain. I don't believe there was better basketball player and human being than the man I called Norman (his middle name). There was no one I competed with harder and had more respect for than him. Just before Wilt died in October 1999, he and I were having one of our marathon telephone calls. Wilt simply loved to talk, and it was impossible to stop him when he got going. I used to kid him by saying, "Norman, you could talk a dog off a meat truck!" Wilt was a Renaissance man in the truest sense of the word. His interests, his knowledge, his experience, and his talents far transcended basketball. Get him started on the stock market or rare Chinese tableware or the mating habits of gnus and you'd never hear the end of it. But in this particular phone call, Wilt was going on and on about a movie project he was involved in, one that was going to be about him. He went on in detail about how seeing from one angle would open up other angles that people might not be ready for . . . and so on. But most important, he explained that the reason he was doing this was because he felt that the only accurate portrait of himself could be done by himself.

I remember saying, "Norman, no one understands you like you. Thank heavens!" When he stopped laughing, he said, "You're right!" But in the next breath he said, "Felton [my middle name and his nickname for me], we are in the same situation." But I immediately thought of a book, because I couldn't imagine who would play me in my movie. That thought caused me to break up.

Wilt said, "What's so funny?"

I told him that when I was doing a talk show in Los Angeles, I had had Rod Steiger on as a guest. I had asked him, "Are you a good actor?"

"I am a great actor," he answered.

I said, "How good?"

"The best."

"If you really think you are that good, I have the ultimate defining role that would leave no uncertainty that you could reach any height as an actor. Could you play me?" He fell off the sofa laughing hysterically. And so did Wilt.

Why a book? Because it will be a gateway to understanding our legendary team and why we were so good. I had opened myself up in two best-sellers, *Go Up for Glory* in 1966 and *Second Wind* in 1979. Both books were memoirs that looked at what the world was like for one individual man at different points in his life, and I didn't feel that there was anything else to tell. Wilt often said, "Man, no one knows more about winning than you do."

After that conversation, and Wilt's sudden and painfully sad exit from my life, I made up my mind that I would go ahead with one last book, and it would go behind the scenes and into the hearts and minds of those with Celtic Pride: my teammates and me. And as if I needed to know that I had made the right choice, my grandson proved to me that I had. During Christmas, 2000, my grandson, sitting at the dinner table amid all the chatter and laughter, coughed and then said with that wonderful childlike innocence, "Grandpa, I have a question to ask you." The table grew silent. "Grandpa, were you as good as Michael Jordan?"

We all laughed except for my grandson. He looked around with that "What's so funny about that?" look. I laughed harder than anyone else and got up from the table and immediately took him out of my will.

In my most half-serious face, I said to my grandson, "You've got the question backwards!" I thought the house would come down. My son explained to my grandson what I meant. But it was a reminder of what most sports fans believe these days. The Boston Celtics are a myth. They were some ancient team that played before the advent of color television. There are generations of young people, kids and others, who don't know anything about the greatest team in sports history and how they achieved what they did. They haven't heard about the principles and values that went into winning eleven NBA Championships in thirteen years. They do not know that I won the NCAA championship, an Olympic gold medal, and the NBA Championship *all in the same year.* So this book is for them as much as it is for those of you who grew up with or cheered the legendary Boston Celtics.

Now, Michael Jordan is an incredible basketball player. I have never seen anyone better. But let me answer one question that many have asked me over the past decade: "Bill, how do you think the Celtics of your era [don't you just love the antiquarian ring to that!] would have done against Michael Jordan and the Chicago Bulls of the nineties?" The Celtics would have won in a walk. We won all those championships in part because we knew how to let other teams' stars do their thing and at the same time take that style of play and convert it to our advantage. My battles with Wilt; our series against the great Bob Pettit; the games we played against "The Big O," Oscar Robertson, one of the greatest players ever; and, of course, our rivalry with the Lakers, led by Jerry West and Elgin Baylor, before and after Wilt got there—all had to do with our knowing how to win games against the very best. We knew how to play our best and how to win against other teams. I'll come back to that, but as it relates to the Bulls, we would let Michael get his forty or fifty points and we would have beaten them decisively. Why? We had the more complete team. We had the matchups, we were far stronger off the bench, the vaunted defense of the Bulls would have been useless against us because of the kind of ball movement and shooting accuracy we regularly brought to our games. Sam Jones was as great a shooter as our game has seen; it would not have been possible to stop him without seriously compromising the defense. Bob Cousy could not have been contained; K.C. Jones, Frank Ramsey, John Havlicek, Tommy Heinsohn—all of them Hall of Famers—would have been waiting like alligators in the shallows to take advantage of any overplaying or shifting by the Bulls. I sincerely believe there was an honest truth behind all those kind words about the Celtics and about me being the greatest of winners.

Basketball is more than a game, it's a metaphor. For me the basketball court was a place where I could bring my thoughts and my understanding of psychology, physiology, mathematics, and, most important, human values.

So what is this book about? It's about the skill sets, mostly mental and emotional, necessary for winning. Winning is an acquired habit; when you win over a long period of time, there are a couple of words you throw out: *luck* and *accident*. For example, in my years with the Celtics, we won a lot of close games. But to win the close games you have to be positioned to win them. We believed that if we were within four or five points with a minute to go, we could win. To make this even more specific: on our team, all of us—from the coach to the last guy on the bench—understood that the key shots at the end of the game were almost always going to be made by one player, Sam Jones. Every team needs a "go to" person, and Sam was ours. To win we knew we had to create the opportunity for him to take those shots . . . nothing good happens by accident. It had to do with knowing our team—and ourselves—so well that we nearly always had the right guys in the right place at the right time. It took every one of us doing what he had to do to make sure that happened. No matter where you are in life, you cannot win consistently unless you are in a position to win.

A basketball team is a controlled unit. The court has a boundary, the game has rules and regulations that everyone who plays must follow. When I was a junior varsity player in high school, we had a coach named George Powles. Powles was the school's baseball coach and had been very successful, but he knew nothing about basketball when the team was turned over to him. The first thing Powles did when he took over was to get a rule book and all the books he could find about basketball. All three books were in our school library. He went over and over the rules, learning everything he could. Then, the first time he met us, he sat us down in the gym and told us what was going on: that he wasn't a basketball coach, that he knew nothing about the game, and that the only way he would be able to help us was by using the rule book. So he made us learn the rules. We had to understand some of the obvious rules—such as no double dribbling, the three-second violation, etc.—but also rules that weren't so obvious, such as air dribbling (you can bounce a ball over an opponent and continue dribbling), or you can dribble with your left hand, bounce it over to your right hand, and it's perfectly okay. In those days, offensive goaltending was permitted. The rules, even more than telling me what I couldn't do, told me what I could do. The more I understood them, the more I was able to use the rules to my advantage.

After deciding to write this book, I realized I would use the idea of lessons and rules I had incorporated into every one of my championships as a framework for this book. Each chapter of *Russell Rules* will be devoted to a lesson that is essential to winning. Within each chapter are three rules that will help you with your leadership skills.

Also, I have taken the liberty, throughout the book, to highlight key phrases and sentences that you may find helpful. The Celtic teams I played for were a model of how a successful enterprise can operate. We used the rules, too. Red Auerbach knew the rule book inside out and constantly used it to his advantage. The controlled environment of the game allowed the Celtics to show what any successful organization can do when there is leadership, planning, execution, and, above all, an ability to respond moment by moment to whatever situation comes up. This book will talk a lot about how the Celtics functioned as a team; there will be a lot of looking back, but the goal will always be to look at what might work for you in the present.

I want to make clear that when I talk about the Boston Celtics of my time, I mean to dispel all of those notions that have since portrayed us in mythical or magical terms. We were not taller, stronger, or mightier than others, the league wasn't weaker (in fact, because there were only eight teams in the league at one point, only the best players played). We didn't have a secret playbook we memorized to baffle our opponents. We were dedicated professionals who did our jobs very, very well. From the owner, Walter Brown, to Red Auerbach, our coach, down to the guy who swept the locker room, there was first and last an unspoken understanding that all of us were there for one purpose: winning. The organization did whatever it was going to take. They weren't going to be constrained in their imagination by the social mores of the time, inhibited by precedent, or restricted from out-of-the-box thinking. It was about creating a team dedicated to one purpose: winning.

The Celtic players from those championship years all have rings that we designed together. On those rings are two words—*teamwork* and *pride*. This book will have much to say about the lessons in teamwork. Teamwork is a subject that many have pontificated about. In this book, you may be startled by the Boston Celtic definition of teamwork. And pride. The epilogue of this book focuses on how to convert Celtic Pride into the culture of your company, business, household, or relationships. I've never forgotten that the rings on my fingers and the rings on the fingers of guys who were last off the bench are the same. From the day I first met my teammates and coach, I experienced something very different from what I had before: a real family whom we all called team. I'll never forget, in my first game, I was called for goaltending and Red Auerbach in a flash was on his feet, screaming at the refs. He took this action for a number of reasons. One, to make sure the referee was sure about the rules of goaltending. He hoped to get a different call the next time. Red also wanted everyone in the building to know that he would fight for his players—me included. Following Red's example, we all stood up for each other.

> *"Celtic Pride" is a real concept, a culture, and a practice rather than an idea. We lived it and breathed it. But we were each responsible for it. It began with a collective determination never to embarrass ourselves.*

In the thirteen years I played and coached for the Celtics, I never heard the words *dynasty* or *legend* spoken by anyone within the organization. The reality is, any team that thinks of itself as a dynasty will never become one. Red used to tell us that what we did last season was important only in terms of what it made our opponents think of us. There were no "winning streaks" on the Celtics. Every game was a new game. We tried to win games one quarter at a time. If we got down three games to one in the play-offs, we never thought of "coming back," only of the next game. In 1968, after the fourth game in the divisional finals, we were down three games to one against the Sixers. As I began my pregame talk before the start of the fifth game, I was talking about assignments and how we were going to beat the Sixers. Mal Graham, a rookie on our team (and today one of Massachusetts's finest and most respected jurists), told me later that he was thinking to himself, "What's he talking about? We are going to get killed. These guys are going to beat the heck out of us." But as a rookie, he didn't yet understand or know about the Celtics and Celtic Pride. What we had at that particular time was a plan and the players who could execute the plan, and he learned before that series was over what being a Celtic was really about. The Celtics went on to stage one of the great comebacks in NBA history as we beat the Sixers in seven games. I see Mal each season when I am with the team in Boston, and he just loves telling that story.

Because teams are made up of individuals, each with his or her own temperament, outlook, sets of values, and beliefs, there will always be a certain inevitable tension within the unit. But successful teams are always able to handle that tension, to incorporate it, use it to advantage. That was a hallmark of my teams. There could never have been anything like Celtic Pride without the respect each of us had for each other—and for the differences between us.

We also enjoyed each other. It's true that some successful organizations can exist without members liking each other, but the comfort level on the Celtics made it easier for us to accept each other's strengths and liabilities so that playing together was more like an adventure than a chore.

To me, the most important part of winning is joy. You can win without joy, but winning that's joyless is like eating in a four-star restaurant when you're not hungry. Joy is a current of energy in your body, like chlorophyll or sunlight, that fills you up and makes you naturally want to do your best. I learned about joy (and about doing my best) early in my life. I would go to my grandfather's house and I would start running and jumping along the way. Later on, when I began to play basketball, I knew that running and jumping—the heart of the game—came from a child's joy. One of the things that the Celtics were able to do was play like children without being childish.

> *All winning streaks begin with a single victory. All successful people, teams, companies, experience their success by an ability to grow, to move from level one to the next, never taking shortcuts, never thinking about more than what's required to make things work right where they are.*

I am frequently asked if I am a basketball player, and I always say no. One time years ago John Havlicek and I were standing in an airport when he asked me why I did that. I told him what I had been telling myself all along: basketball is what I do, it's not who I am.

Before we begin our journey through the eleven lessons on leadership and winning, I want to pass along a first rule.

A few years ago, I was in the locker room of the Phoenix Suns when I noticed a sign over the door that led to the arena. The players would pass under this sign before the start of every game. The sign said:

> *"The game's on the schedule, we have to play it, we might as well win it."*
> **—Bill Russell**

COMMITMENT
BEGINS WITH
CURIOSITY

A S A LIFETIME OBSERVER OF SOCIAL TRENDS, I WAS FASCI-
nated during the nineties to see how commitment, or
the struggle with making and keeping commitments, was one
of those cliché-ridden concepts that seemed to define the
decade. Television and movies were filled with characters who
couldn't follow their hearts and make commitments or stand
behind the ones they made.

Everyone has a pretty good idea that success in business, as
much as in life, requires commitment to a goal or mission, an
ideal or standard, or, at the very least, another person. But first,
commitment begins with the one who is looking back at you in
the mirror. When it is hesitancy looking back at you, you know
you are still looking for commitment.

Recently, I had the chance to speak at a Tony Robbins
seminar. Fifteen thousand folks were giving up a day, paying a
substantial registration fee, to learn how to change their lives
for the better. Tony said something powerful about commitment that day: "I believe life is constantly testing us for our
level of commitment, and life's greatest rewards are reserved for

those who demonstrate a never-ending commitment to act until they achieve. This level of resolve can move mountains, but it must be constant and consistent." As simplistic as this sounded, commitment in my mind is the common denominator separating those who live their dreams from those who live their lives regretting the opportunities they have squandered. So what's the tiebreaker? What differentiates those who see and pursue the power of commitment versus those who can't? One word: *curiosity*. Curiosity is as common as the air we breathe, but it is also the oxygen of accomplishment and success.

Here are some basic Russell Rules on curiosity to get us started:

RUSSELL RULES

Rule One: Good questions are more important than easy answers. The "silly question" is often not silly at all, it's the beginning of a new pathway toward a solution. I remember reading that when Einstein was asked what was the secret of his success, he unhesitatingly replied, "The most important thing is not to stop the questioning." Throughout my life, I have been fascinated by Leonardo da Vinci and Michelangelo. They knew the power of that most important word in any language. All great inventions, new ideas, works of art, are based on curiosity. Millions saw apples fall off trees, but it was Newton who asked, "Why?"

Rule Two: Curiosity is a process. I wrote a magazine article years ago entitled "Life Is a Journey, Not a Destination." It was fundamentally about creating a driving force in your life, understanding that force and always challenging it through self-evaluation and questioning. In other words, one of the most important characteristics one must possess for success in a world that is predicated on the survival of the fittest is an interest in life, good, bad, or peculiar.

Rule Three: Curiosity should always be challenging and always solidify a sense of commitment. The goal is to solve the problem, to win the game, to get past the place where you might have been stuck. The goal of winning slips away with the loss of curiosity. Though curiosity is a child's possession, an adult can use it consciously as a tool, can develop it in the building of a winning strategy. It does not matter if the game is running a Fortune 500 company or a family, curiosity leads to understanding (your competition, your colleagues, your family) and ultimately to the implementation of goals. Curiosity should be a verb, not a noun. Curiosity is connected to doing, to solving, experimenting, trying, failing, and then accomplishing. "How does this work?" "What do I do?" "What happens next?" "What do I do to make this turn out the way I want—or the way you want?" "How do I get from here to there?" "What can I do to help you (or myself)?" Those are all basic questions that stem from curiosity, but that are also basic to winning.

When commitment is coerced, thinking is not required—just obedience. Curiosity on the other hand is the arch-stone of that thinking process that leads to doing. When I was a child, soon after my family had moved from Louisiana to West Oakland, California, my mother decided that I had to have a library card. I spent my time poring over art books, particularly over reproductions of the work of Michelangelo and Leonardo and the other Renaissance painters. I remember that I'd sit up at a table near the stacks, opening the books, staring at one plate after another. I began to play a game with myself. After I'd looked at the paintings for a long enough time, I'd close my eyes and see if I could remember every detail of what I had just looked at. If I couldn't, I'd study the painting again until I thought I got it right. Then I played another game. I wouldn't bring books home from the library just because I was curious to see if I could draw out what I had memorized. I'd sit at home and try to copy on paper what was in my brain. Most of the lines and the dimensions were correct, but I somehow missed the paintings completely. I realized—as a kid—that what these artists had that I didn't have was a distinctive quality, a kind of signature statement. In Michelangelo, for example, fingers have an absolutely original look. Whether the fingers are fat or skinny, long or short, no one else but Michelangelo could have painted them. There was a signature style to them.

The way I took to Leonardo and Michelangelo was eventually how I took to the game of basketball. As a young player, my abilities didn't drop down from heaven. I didn't see a basketball until I was about nine, and then when I began playing in high school, initially I wasn't a starter on my team. When I graduated, however, I was chosen to be part of a team of California high school all-stars that was going to tour western Canada. I was picked only because I had graduated in midyear and other players from my school—which had a championship team—weren't available. For me, however, it was an incredible opportunity.

The game as it was played then was really static; it was nowhere near the kind of mobile style that has taken over today's game. The only time players were supposed to leave their feet was for rebounds, which north of the border were called caroms. The standard shots were the set shot and a running layup. Jump shots were an emerging innovation because a player had to go airborne to make them.

Our coach was Brick Swegle, who had a sense of fun and a willingness to let his players basically do what they wanted. If they felt like jump-shooting or leaving their feet, so be it. Same on defense, where the belief was that any defender who left his feet was out of position. Swegle, in effect, gave me the green light to use my curiosity to explore the game that so fascinated me. My commitment to basketball and eventual love of the game came directly from taking advantage of this opportunity. Curiosity was leading me forward.

From town to town, I watched incessantly two of my teammates, Bill Treu, from Los Angeles High School, and Eural McKelvey, from Richmond High School. Each was a totally different kind of player. I'm sure I wore their ears off trying to find out the secrets of how they played the game. Treu was a ball handler the likes of which weren't seen in those days. He never did anything predictably; when he moved—with or without the ball—it was impossible to keep up with him. A defender's feet would become hopelessly tangled, yet Treu was as fluid and graceful as he was deceptive; he could thread his way through a mass of defenders as if his body were quicksilver. McKelvey was a rebounder who thought about rebounding the way architects made measurements for rooftops and domes. He was into angles, floor position, when and how to leave his feet. I did something else, too. Sitting there on the bus, I'd close my eyes and try to see each move these players made the same way I had "memorized" Michelangelo and Leonardo. As I saw them move in my mind's eye, I imagined myself as their shadow or mirror image. Every movement, every subtle gesture they made, I made in reverse, till I knew that I could guard them both.

In college, I played in a program that was very successful. We won two consecutive NCAA championships at the University of San Francisco during the fifties, winning fifty-five consecutive games in the process. But my focus there was narrow, my sense of commitment limited. My teammates were older and did not seem very accepting of me. In my sophomore season, we were an ordinary team. Our record was 14-7 and the graduating seniors made a point of letting me know that without them the team was going to fall apart. It did just the oppo-

When I joined the varsity, I had replaced a senior, a big, slow center who could barely get his hand over the rim. I could run backward faster than he could run forward. Sometimes, in the gym, just for fun, I'd try jumping to see how high I could go. I could get my eyes higher than the level of the rim. And, I used to be able to kick the bottom of the net. But my coach insisted that I play just as the senior had. My coach wanted me to position myself, rebound, plant myself in the middle, just like my predecessor. I could, but I wouldn't do that. I was learning another game, my curiosity was leading me elsewhere.

site. But I had the feeling that all the while I was swimming up-stream. My coach—who became a dear friend for life afterward—never once complimented me on my game and, I believe, never really saw all the positive things that I was doing on the court. He was brought up in the old school. When he saw me leave my feet on defense, he believed I had overcommitted my-self; when he saw me move the ball like a guard, he thought I was taking unnecessary chances. I wasn't.

One of my college teammates, later to become a teammate on the Celtics, was K.C. Jones. K.C., in addition to being one of the most intelligent basketball players I've ever known, was also a very decent and caring human being. One time when I was a freshman, he saw me walking around with holes in my shoes. He wanted to know why my shoes were like that. I told him I had no money. K.C. took his scholarship allowance, went out, and bought me a pair of shoes! But K.C. was more than a loyal friend, he was someone with whom I could share my curiosity about basketball with. The two of us created a two-man laboratory on the court.

We used to spend hour after hour talking and practicing, figuring things out. This became a verbal extension of what I had learned from watching Treu and McKelvey. We were figur-ing how to time plays and passes, and how to effectively run patterns; how to give a fake and move on without waiting for the opponent to take the fake; how to present a target to each other; what kind of velocity you should make on passes; and what kind of pass is the best to make under specific circum-stances. We realized early in our discussions that you should never pass a ball to a seven-footer below his knees. Most often, players missed short.

During the summers, we would often play pickup games.

We'd never allow ourselves to be on the same team. Competitively it would have made for one-sided games, but most of all it would rob us of the curiosity we were both actively employing to improve. I wanted to guard K.C. when we played so I could learn the moves of a smaller, quicker man. I wanted to shadow him, become his mirror. I wanted him to guard me because one of the really difficult problems for a big man in the post is learning how to protect the ball, to hold on to it, to pass the ball under extreme pressure. Other big men challenge you with their height, their reach. But smaller players, guards, will attack the ball, they'll reach in and try to swipe the ball from you. They're quicker than big men, they use their hands, their ability to shift position and harass. For me, learning K.C.'s moves meant becoming quicker, more agile. That was my game—and it was very different from other centers'. My learning was driven by endless curiosity, paying attention to what players did, what their idiosyncracies were, discovering their "signature styles."

When I got to the Celtics, I could do a lot more than rebound. The Celtics had wanted me to fill that missing hole in their attack, to get the ball off the boards and get it to one of their guards. Before my very first game, Red Auerbach, walking down the tunnel toward the court with me, asked if I had any worries about my ability to score. "I wouldn't say I had any worries, I think about it sometimes," I said. He told me then he'd make a deal with me, that he'd never use statistics in negotiating one of my contracts, that the only thing he'd ever bring up was how I played. I welcomed what he said. It took a lot of the pressure off and it also freed me to play my game, which went beyond rebounding. I was comfortable running plays, setting up, passing the ball, working to get my teammates good shots, and so my task, I knew then, was to figure out how to make all that happen.

> **What I found with the Celtics was a set of other players who were brilliant and accomplished. I needed to know who the different players were, what their tendencies were, their habits, their preferences. I had to learn about their thinking, their temperaments. For me to play my best game, I had to discover theirs.**

The Celtics were noted as a fast-breaking team, although our game plan was to start with defense first. Even though our defense triggered our offense, a couple of years we averaged over 120 points a game, which is unthinkable today. None of us ever saw a shot we didn't like. But the fast break, which created this kind of scoring, was a problem for me for a time. I could run the break like a point guard going right up the middle, weaving in and out of traffic. I had all of the necessary moves set in muscle memory. Other players would say to me, often with looks of amazement on their face, that they didn't know I could be that agile. This, of course, pleased me. But then, one night, while I was leading a break up the floor, I noticed Bob Cousy over my shoulder, running behind me. I told myself something was wrong, the picture was out of whack, the signature style was missing. Bob Cousy, to this day, is the best I've ever seen in the NBA at running a fast break. What I was inadvertently doing was taking him out of his game, out of what he did best. My curiosity was getting the better of me. In my search to learn all I could about my teammates, I started to learn how to play like them. I needed to know their games inside out without actually doing what they were doing. That would actually have hurt our team. Cousy never said anything to me about it, Red never said anything, reporters never criticized me. I realized how easy it had been to undermine my team's game by doing my own thing. What I did after that was to give Cousy the ball as soon as I got it and then fill the lane so he could go to work. That way I was helping him to play his game, which was exactly what our team needed.

Children have an easier time with curiosity because so much of what happens to them is brand-new. They can go from one thing to the other without ever asking themselves if there is anything they need to do. A lot of times there isn't. When my family left Louisiana, for example, we went by train. The whole world opened up for me. The first stop the train made was Little Rock, Arkansas, and then we went to St. Louis and got a streamliner heading for Denver and then the West Coast. There was so much to soak up. All the new sights and sounds: the Rocky Mountains, the deserts. And then the train wasn't segregated. My mind, my imagination, jumped from one thing to the other, without any thought of needing to do something. But curiosity when it leads to commitment means consciously figuring out what needs to be done to accomplish a goal or task. If a child is crying, a responsible parent will find out why and do something about it; if a patient is ill, a doctor relies on his ability to make a diagnosis before he takes action; if things aren't working on a team, a good, dedicated player will always seek to find out why and try to correct it.

How do you put curiosity to work in your life? What practical steps can you take to make sure you exploit this natural power to allow you to make commitments? The most basic step is a willingness to deal with what is right in front of you. If your competitor has a product that is top of the line, you have to find out what made that product so special before you commit yourself to surpassing him. That is what VHS technology did to Betamax. What can I do? Say that to yourself, teach yourself to keep saying it in every situation that matters. The answers will come—and with them real commitment—even if, for a time, the self-questioning might seem to slow you down.

The Sony corporation is as successful a giant as there is in the electronics business. Years ago, when the company began, it was not a giant. It produced transistor radios. The company was the brainchild of a single man who was endlessly curious about the way radios, TVs, and stereo systems worked. When television sets began to be mass-produced in the forties and fifties, my understanding is this company, to compete, held back. The head of the company understood that the visual spectrum of early TVs was primitive and could be greatly improved. The first color sets, he observed, were poor, the colors distorted. By waiting and experimenting, Sony came up with something called the Trinitron, a set that revolutionized color television. The company, as a result, boomed. The company had further success when it produced the Walkman. People today can clip on headsets that make them feel they're in a concert hall. But the first headsets by rival companies were tinny and not very promising. Sony's CEO just happened to love music. He held his product off the marketplace until his engineers could figure out what it would take to produce concert-hall sound. Successful companies are always putting curiosity to use in that way. Boeing has constantly been able to keep up with

rivals in producing giant aircraft because it long ago incorporated curiosity in its operation in the form of a powerful R&D
division. American car companies, which, for a time, seemed
to have been shouldered off the road by Japanese imports, have
made a tremendous comeback by taking the time to learn what
they had to do to come up with a comparable product. In every
life situation we find ourselves in, we can open ourselves or defeat ourselves by recognizing—or refusing to recognize—our
own curiosity. What can I do? Keep asking the question until
the answers come.

When I think of commitment—and success—I think of
my father. After the war, when we were living in Oakland, he
lost his job in the shipyards. Workers in defense plants all over
the country found themselves unemployed. So my father, who
had a family to look after, said to himself, what can I do? He
bought an army surplus truck and went out to farmers in the
country, asking one after the other if they needed someone to
bring in their crops. Many of them said they did. My father
then went home and put up a sign near his truck that said that
he would transport anyone to the country who wanted to pick
fruit. The truck left at six, would return in the evening; he'd
take the guys out to these farms, drop them off, pick them up—
and charge them a buck for the ride out and back. So, right
away, he had a regular daily income of about twenty or thirty
dollars. Then he charged each farmer a dollar for every worker
he brought in. And then sometimes he'd stay and be the field
boss and he'd charge ten dollars for that. Then, on top of that,
he'd get so much for every box that was picked. After a while,
my father had a fleet of four or five guys with trucks and was
doing very well. He had figured out what he had to do to maintain his commitment to his family and to himself.

Commitment means a willingness to put up with adversity, uncertainty, even failure. My father never had a guarantee that his trucking venture would succeed. He started out broke and had to have wondered if buying that first truck wasn't a little extravagant. It didn't matter. His curiosity—taking things one step at a time—led him to success. What he was committed to was clear—same as with the chairman of Sony or the CEO of Boeing or Red Auerbach.

> **As long as you have a willingness to accept adversity and do something about it, you give yourself the chance to win. When your curiosity asks you to take risks, take them.**

When I walked into the Celtics locker room for the first time, I saw a bunch of guys, each of whom I knew by sight. In fact, I had read everything I could about every guy on the Celtics and in the league. I knew what every opponent would look like before I played against them. What I was interested in was winning and playing my game—with these guys—and I didn't know how that was going to evolve. But it almost didn't matter, because I was committed to winning with whatever team I was playing with.

But because I was late joining the team (having taken a few weeks off after the Olympics to get married), I didn't start the first twelve games. As a result, I was able to study my new teammates, take in their different styles, and just watch how they played, moved, and thought. Watching the games, I would see what moves I would need to play with them—and to have them play with me. But still, I didn't know yet what I would have to do. That came strictly from playing.

The same with the other guys on the team. Our team focus was always about exploring the best things we could get out of each other on the court. There was never a question of feeling whether or not I fit in. That was taken care of from the start. When I got to Boston, Walter Brown, Red Auerbach, and Bill Sharman met me at the airport. The gesture didn't need to be made but was—and it let me know I was welcome. From Walter Brown, the owner, down to the last guy on the bench, all anyone seemed interested in was that I was a ballplayer, and the only question in the air was how good I might be and how we would all fit in a successful system. What followed was the really important part of the story, the part that was all about curiosity.

The Celtic "system" was designed to permit intelligent, winning players to endlessly use their own curiosity and creativity to accomplish results. That was why each of the players felt such an extraordinary commitment to the team. It was a living, everyday thing, a practice far more than a promise, it was their team.

Our system, just because it was so endlessly inventive, was deceptive to other teams and players. One time, a group of NBA all-stars went on tour behind the Iron Curtain. Red was our coach. Before the first game, players huddled and one of them wanted to know what plays we should use. One of our team's stars, Hall-of-Famer Bob Pettit of the Hawks, said, "Let's use the Celtic plays, we all know them!" He was right—but he didn't understand all the nuances of our plays.

I want to make sure what I'm saying isn't misunderstood, so let's review. Russell's Rules for Curiosity are as simple as the Celtic plays:

RUSSELL RULES

Rule One: Ask questions. A silly question is worth any number of easy answers.

Rule Two: Remember that curiosity is a process, and it is not a solution in itself. It's ongoing and always leaves it to you to figure out what you need to do next.

Rule Three: To really be committed, you must always pursue the questions until you get meaningful answers.

As I have come to understand curiosity as an active, working part of my life, it has led me to some important conclusions about commitment I might not have reached otherwise. What must be done to achieve success is often something where the doer is not the direct beneficiary. This is especially true for any kind of team player. Trying to figure out how something is done automatically pushes one toward commitment. That commitment can be to making yourself the best parent you can be, the best teacher, the best golfer. Commitment to a collective entity like the Boston Celtics or Boeing inevitably means a commitment to a team. But whatever the nature of the commitment, the deepest is the one that comes from within yourself and that is freely given.

One last word about curiosity. After I had been with the Celtics for some years, I decided to take a trip to Africa. My goal was to see some of the different countries and people—but also to teach basketball to youngsters who I knew had no idea of the game. I had this picture in my head of kids who were like me when I arrived in Oakland and had never seen a basketball before. I wanted to hold clinics for kids. I had no illusions about what I could do in a short while, but I did think I could provoke curiosity in some kids so that they might then teach themselves about the game and perhaps find in it some of the joy and success I had found for myself.

I stopped in Ethiopia when that country was in the midst of a weeklong national celebration. There were athletic competitions, parades, and dancing. It was a perfect time to hold basketball clinics for kids. I stopped in local villages, places that weren't even on the map, and I tried to show these local children some of the basics of the game, just to get them interested. They were. They had no idea who I was, but they flocked around me, asking all kinds of questions. One after the other, the kids kept asking me how did this or that work, why did you have to dribble the ball, what was the best way to dribble, why couldn't you dribble the ball, stop, dribble again? Why did the tallest player need to play closest to the basket? As the clinics continued, the questions got more complicated. How could you get a player free to shoot the ball if the players guarding him were especially good? What was a fast break and what would happen if you tried it and it didn't work? The children soaked up the game as fast as I could teach it. There was no tradition of basketball in Ethiopia, but it did not matter because the kids were so caught up in it. In time, if the game was made a regular part of their lives, commitment and success would have been inevitable. We would be seeing Ethiopian stars in the game as surely as we are seeing European stars in the game today.

My trip attracted wide attention. The emperor, Haile Selassie himself, took note of it and one day asked me to explain why I was there. We met at a parade ground where national games and celebrations were being held. I was summoned to His Majesty's presence by one of his aides. Selassie was waiting for me in a limousine (because, I was told later, he did not want to be seen standing next to someone as tall as I was).

The emperor spoke to me in English, and I realized immediately what a compliment that was. Heads of state always speak in their first language—but he had chosen to speak in mine! We sat there and talked for about fifteen minutes. He wanted to know why I had come to Ethiopia, what was I doing, what did I have in mind? I told him that I was going from area to area, school to school, introducing kids to basketball. Why? he wanted to know. I had come to Ethiopia by myself—no teammates, no State Department entourage. The look on his face was curious—he seemed actively interested in what I had to say. I mentioned how important I thought it was for kids to have one time in their life when they simply were able to have fun. He nodded. Then I told him how important I thought curiosity was, how natural it was in children. With that, the emperor's expression seemed to change. The look on his face seemed to soften; his eyes, which had been searching me out, looking for motives that had been elusive, imperceptibly sharpened.

"Aha," he said, "curiosity. Of course!"

LESSON TWO

$$Ego = MC^2$$

I N MARCH 1999, I WAS IN BOSTON FOR THE ANNOUNCEMENT of the May tribute to re-retire my number. The Celtics asked me if I would speak to the present team, which, at that point, were on a nine-game losing streak and were not playing together as a unit. You may be thinking, how does a guy old enough to be a modern player's grandfather connect and communicate with guys on that team? The answer is in finding common ground.

I began by telling them that despite that so much had been written about me being the most unselfish player, I was the most egotistical player they would ever meet. All kinds of nervous smiles were coming back at me from people who were not sure what was coming next. These smiles disappeared when I said, "Do you know the difference between your ego and mine? My ego is not a personal ego, it's a team ego. My ego demands— for myself—the success of my team. My personal achievement became my team achievement. The single greatest disappointment in my career was when I was hurt and we didn't win a twelfth title." These talented young players all looked at me with strange expressions on their faces. I could almost read their minds. Here was Bill Russell, the guy with eleven championship rings on his ten fingers, telling them that the only thing that mattered to him was how his team did. But that's exactly what I was saying. Thirty-plus years later, the only regrets I have are about those two years when the Celtics didn't win. My career was never about personal statistics. It was never about contracts or money. I never paid attention to MVP awards or how many endorsements I had lined up—only how many titles we won. My team went out night after night, played totally unselfishly and had fun.

In team efforts, individual ego can be detrimental and devisive, and unfortunately we see it too often around us in our society and culture. In sports it's defined by rewarding individual achievement in team sports.

So, how do you build team ego? Here are my three Russell Rules:

RUSSELL RULES

Rule One: Establish your business culture around your team. A business culture in its simplest form is nothing more than the environment in which decisions are made. All business cultures, all families, succeed or fail on the basis of the decisions they make. So the concept of team ego is a factor in getting individuals to see success not in terms of individual performance but rather in getting more fulfillment from the group's success.

Rule Two: Vest people in the process. Help everyone on the team understand where the group is going, how it is going to get there, and, most important, why sharing decision-making is a critical step in achieving team ego. For example, most companies in America do not share their financial or budgeting processes with anyone in the company except the senior managers. I've always been impressed with those companies that practice what is called open-book management. Since everyone's paycheck depends on the team's success, why not have everyone on the team fully understand how much it costs the company to make products or provide services? Understanding these "details" will empower folks to do their part to benefit the team.

Rule Three: Create unselfishness as the most important team characteristic. I remember once speaking to a group of top salespeople—not the whole sales force, only the ones who had excelled. I remember raising some eyebrows when I said I was speaking to the wrong audience. Those who needed lessons in motivation and winning were the ones I needed to talk to but who weren't there. But I went on to say to them, "Next year, your job is to work together to ensure that every salesperson makes it to these awards presentations. Your job is to wake up in the morning and say, 'What can I do to help those I work with succeed? What can I do today to make the team better?' " The response I got was one of the most enthusiastic I have ever received on the lecture trail.

When I played, I was the most dominant player in the game. But I was so team-oriented that I never needed to prove it. All I wanted was for my attitude to rub off on my teammates, and it did. Many people forget that I played the most important role in that "unforgettable" game where "Havlicek stole the ball!" in the seventh game of the Divisional Finals against the Sixers in 1965. Of course, I'm kidding—but remember what happened? There were seconds to go and the Celtics are up by one and John stole the inbounds pass to win the game. Every highlight shows the play with Johnny Most screaming, "Havlicek stole the ball! Havlicek stole the ball!" But what folks may not remember is that it was my throw in seconds before that had hit one of the guide wires holding the backboard that had given the Sixers a chance to win. Just before that moment, we had gotten possession of the ball and called time-out. I went into the huddle and said, "I'll make the inbounds pass!" I did not trust anyone but me to make that inbounds pass, and my coach and teammates went along. So what happened? I hit the guide wire, giving our opponents a chance to beat us. We went back into the huddle and I remember saying, "Hey, we got to do something!" I knew, because of our team ego, everyone was thinking the same thought . . . "What can I do to help win this game?" And John did just that.

> *Being remembered for winning eighteen championships in twenty-one years, including eleven NBA titles in thirteen seasons, and being picked by the players in the league as a five-time MVP is more important than any individual record. For me, winning as a team is not a coincidence, it is a choice. In the end, you are judged by winning.*

We always needed each other, and we could always count on one another because we had taken such pains over such a long period to build the strength of our togetherness as a team.

When *Sports Illustrated* named me the "Greatest Team Winner of the Twentieth Century," it was rewarding because someone noticed. I will always prefer to be remembered as Bill Russell, captain of the Boston Celtics.

I realized at a young age that winning was the ultimate form of athletic expression. And to win regularly, I would have to subordinate my individual goals so my team would be able to win. As a result, I became the kind of leader who understood that doing the most for my team would best guarantee success. To get there, I had to get past a lot of things that weren't really vital to winning but that made me feel good—like taking shots. I can't emphasize this enough.

I first learned this lesson as a sophomore at the University of San Francisco. That was my breakthrough year as a basketball player. When I started playing varsity basketball at the University of San Francisco, I knew I had some talent. The freshman team I had played for was better than the varsity. In fact, I had heard that a couple of varsity players had let it be known they didn't think I was very good. A starting guard on the team had made a point of telling our coach, with others listening in, that he thought my getting an athletic scholarship was a big waste of money and that it would eventually cost the coach his job. Another player, a forward, who used to tell people that he was going to make all-America that year, ran into me one afternoon in the dorms and, unsolicited, made a point of letting me know he thought I was a lousy basketball player. I was just then scheduled to join the varsity. "Russell," this guy said, "next week you're gonna be playing with the men and I don't think you can cut it." I knew how good I was. I didn't need this guy or anyone else telling me otherwise. In the first game we played, my goal was to do the best I could, because if you're going to spend your career trying to prove yourself to other people, you are bound to fail sooner or later.

Our team then went on a road trip to Wyoming and Utah. Our first game in Laramie was a disaster. We were crushed. Wyoming's two forwards scored twenty and nineteen points respectively (in those days scoring in double figures was a big deal). I was pounded underneath, pushed and pummeled without a single foul being called. The following night we went out and played Brigham Young in Provo, Utah. Early in the game, their big guy, on one play, went to the top of the circle, faked, and as I went up into the air, he dribbled past me for an easy layup. My favorite teammate walked up to me and said, "Why don't you start trying to play some defense, Russell?" I looked at this guy and quietly said, "Okay." What I did then was to close down BYU's center completely. That's all I had on my mind. The guy I was guarding never got another point that night. I blocked shot after shot, I took rebound after rebound from him. But I also didn't block a shot by anyone else or help out on defense in any other way. At halftime we were trailing by twenty-five points. I had two points and my man had two points. That was enough. They had been kicking us around like a tin can. Guys would go by for layups, but I was playing torrid defense on my guy—exclusively. I'd step out of the way when any other player went by me. In the locker room between halves, my coach, Phil Wolpert, said, "What's the matter, Russell, have you been reading your press clippings?"

I did not reply, but thought, "This is not a very good team

and we're not going anywhere. But, I want to be a good basketball player and I'm going to go out and play as hard as I can for as long as I can with no regard to what these people, my teammates, can do. We're not going to win but I'm going to be the best basketball player any of these guys ever saw."

We went out in the second half and I scored twenty-two points and we got Brigham Young's lead down from twenty-five points to three points before they finally beat us. My coach walked away from this game thinking that what he had said had motivated me (I have no idea what was in my teammate's mind). All it did was to make me want to be the most dominant player ever. At the end of the season I realized we had a mediocre 14-7 record, yet we had enough talent to be one of the really great college teams in the country. After that season, I concluded that "I was wrong. I am part of a team and I am not strong enough to change the atmosphere for the better, and the team wasn't strong enough to change me, so we feuded." After that season, I vowed to never again concentrate on individual goals at the expense of the team.

Only when I reached the Celtics did I really come to appreciate the joy of winning as a team. To begin with, the Celtics were the definition of a genuine team. They had been built carefully, player by player, over the years. The players had been chosen not only for their specific skills but because they complemented each other so well. The coach, Red Auerbach, wanted to win as much as any of the players. You couldn't be around him for five minutes without knowing he had as big an ego as anyone. But he always conveyed the sense that his players—and not he—were the ones who went out and played the game.

Red wasn't a great coach because he told himself he

wanted to be great—but because of the way he worked. He had an unfailing sense of the unit on the floor. He knew each of the players as individuals, respected them, and saw them together, as a team. That had nothing to do with his being a good guy (which he was), but was because he burned to win and be seen as the best coach who ever lived (which he was)— and the success of his team was the way he could get there. There were never any pep talks, never any grandstanding (well, there were victory cigars!). All that was required for Red's ego to be filled was for the Celtics to win basketball games and championships.

Nearly all of my new teammates were egotists in exactly the way Red was. Each of them knew how good he was, but each of them seemed to understand perfectly that everyone had to play his part for us to win. Bob Cousy, for example, prided himself on doing all the little subtle things he could to outfox, outsmart, and outscore opponents. But there was never a second's hesitation when it came to setting up open team-mates or to giving up the ball in the last second to Sam Jones to take the shot that would make the back pages the next day. Bill Sharman, as good a guy as you'll ever find, was the same way—completely competitive but at ease with doing whatever he could for his teammates. Tommy Heinsohn wasn't nearly as comfortable in his own skin as Cousy or Sharman, but his ego was just as strong and creative. You could see it especially when his game was off, when his shot from the corner wouldn't fall. Somehow he'd turn himself into a tornado, moving all over the court, trying that much harder to make up for what wasn't working. And as for Frank Ramsey: here was a guy who wasn't a starter, but whose ego was so strong he literally created the concept of the "sixth man" in the basketball world.

When I joined the Celtics, I knew what I could do. I also knew I wanted to win championships. But I was also joining a team I knew little about and that hadn't been my first choice. I didn't automatically link my ego to anyone else's. I didn't know how I'd be received or if the way I saw myself would bother anyone else. I didn't care. I wore facial hair, for instance—a sharp goatee and a thin mustache. Over time, I developed a calculated air of mystery so that my teammates would never be able to take me for granted (or later on to see that I happened to like them). I had a job to do, and what my ego told me then was that I had to take control of how anyone else was going to define me.

Because I didn't join the team until December that year, it took a while before I was starting. My coach, my teammates, were openly friendly—very different from what I had experienced in the Olympics and in college and different from what I had anticipated. Arnie Risen, a talented player, was the starting center when I got there. He went out of his way to be as helpful to me as he could, even though he had to know I was eventually going to be his replacement on the team. I was really impressed by this. Here was a guy who was going to lose his job to me but put what was best for the team first. In fact, Red rewarded Arnie for being so selfless by extending his career.

In the first game I started, I felt that I didn't belong on the floor. I was the team's center, but Red let Cousy move into the pivot on offense because a smaller man was guarding him and Cousy had thought that he would be able to score and get his man in foul trouble. It didn't work. Cousy was beaten half to death before Red decided to move Bill Sharman into the pivot, then Tommy Heinsohn—each time with the same result. We were down by over twenty points when Red called a time-out and brought the team over to stand around him. (The Celtics never sat during time-outs—partly because Red had an iron-clad conviction that standing both kept players from getting tired and also helped intimidate the other team.) I went right to the bench and sat during that time-out.

I was aware that every pair of eyes on the team was on me. I could almost make out the words in the stares: "Red doesn't want you to sit down, rook, you're supposed to stand here with the rest of us!" Red finally asked me what was wrong, why I wasn't in the huddle. I told him:

"I don't need to be in the huddle to know to stay out of the way. I can't play anything but center, and everybody else is playing center so I might as well just sit here." I knew that we would be a better team if I was playing center. Because with me playing center, the forwards being forwards and the guards being guards, we would have better motion than four guys standing around trying to feed the pivot.

But what happened next moved me, and my ego, to another level. Now for a rookie to have said what I had said was, to say the least, unusual, but so was my coach and so was my team. Red turned to the other players and said, "Okay, nobody else go into the pivot." He turned to me: "You play pivot." And

> *To get the most out of being a member of a team it is absolutely essential to establish yourself as an integral part of the unit. That is your responsibility, not anyone else's.*

so I did. He was listening to his players. He used his ego to make the right decision even though he himself had not thought of the answer. He epitomized what a good manager does: he used a good idea from one of his players to make his team win.

By the end of my rookie season, I was in the mix. I wasn't always the first option ever on offense, but I had done what I needed to do. On defense, I became the key player the Celtics had been looking for. But I added my own game—which I liked to call the horizontal game because I did much more than jump to the basket—to what the team did, and the results were a first-ever championship.

The strongest competitive challenge came a couple of seasons later when Wilt Chamberlain joined the league. Until then I had been the league's dominant center, recognized along with Cousy as a pillar of the World Champion Celtics. There was no other team that even came close to challenging us, but then, one day, there was Wilt, all seven feet two inches of him with the basketball skills to match.

There were some good centers in the league then, but there had never been anything like Wilt Chamberlain. For the two and a half seasons I played without him, I could more or less do what I wanted. And then suddenly, there was a man in the middle who towered over me, who was built like Goliath, who had hands that could swallow basketballs, who had the strength to fight his way through double and triple teams to savagely slam a ball home, to gently finger-roll a ball into the basket or to go wide and put the softest shot off the glass, to back off a step and go into the air for a seemingly unstoppable jumper. He understood the fundamentals of rebounding well enough so that with the great physical advantage he had, he was as good a rebounder as the league had seen or will ever see.

In his rookie season, Wilt led the league in scoring, averaging 37.6 points per game. He led the league in rebounding, setting an NBA record at the time both for total rebounds and rebounds per game. What was I to do? How to play him? Here was a test of ego that Machiavelli or Freud might have taken pleasure in devising.

As I came to know him over the years, Wilt was one of the gentlest, kindest people I have ever known—apart from the fierceness of his game. His ego was as large as he was, but it only made him more interesting. His honesty and generosity went hand in hand. I had a standing invitation to his house on Thanksgiving because for years the Celtics wound up playing a turkey-day game in Philadelphia, where he and his family lived. I used to drop in and visit him in later years when he owned Small's Paradise, a club in Harlem. He dressed flashily, loved women and fancy cars—and he loved showing them off. Once, when he bought a lavender-colored Bentley, he drove it all the way up to Boston just to have me come out of my restaurant and see it standing there at the curb like a king's ransom. He knew how much I would enjoy his enjoyment, and he knew me well enough to understand that I would appreciate that he had driven his new trophy all the way from New York to Boston just to show it to me.

The competition with Wilt made me a better player, brought more out of me than if I had been there by myself. I believe to this day our competition was unrivaled in sports.

In 1963, right after Cousy retired, I thought about what goals I wanted to set for myself. At first I told myself it would finally be okay to raise my scoring average by a couple of points, but what was more important for the team was going to be my ability to raise my number of assists. And, I realized that Cousy's absence would mean that everyone else on the team would be looking to shoot more, and I decided to actually cut back on my points per game, so I could be sure other players would become more involved. That's what winning demanded. That's what my ego demanded.

Wilt had one kind of game and I had another. There was no one ever who was as strong to the basket as he was. He exemplified what I call the vertical game, the game from the floor to the rim. You could surround Wilt with three defenders and he could fight his way through them as though they were flies. I remember one time he took a rebound out near the broken line of the foul circle and in one leaping motion jammed the ball home, going over two or three guys who were in the way! My game, the horizontal game, was totally different. I could run the floor, move laterally, block shots, put the ball on the floor, play defense as strongly away from the basket as I did near it. My game had more finesse, I used agility more than power. If I had ever tried to match Wilt in a power game, I would have lost.

Now even though the teams Wilt played for won only two championships, he wanted to win as badly as I did. In an ironic way, his numbers obscured that. He averaged fifty points per game one season. In a single game against the New York Knicks, he poured in one hundred points. People inevitably thought he was playing for himself. But that was never the case.

He had different ideas about winning than I did, but more importantly, we played the position so differently—and he had a different kind of ego. He reasoned, quite logically, that if his teammates got him the ball, if he was able to use all his skills in a single game, his team should win. He was right . . . except when they played us. There was no one on the floor who could stop him. He knew his skills well enough to understand what he could—and couldn't—do. No one could stop his shot. It made no difference if he was double- or triple-teamed, get him the ball and he would score. Let him stay in the middle and other teams would need an earthmover before they would be able to push him aside. He worked harder than any other bas-ketball player I have ever seen. During a game, he'd change his sweat-soaked jersey at half-time. He routinely lost five or ten pounds in forty-eight minutes. And it was all because he was absolutely certain that when he put his team on his shoulders, they had the best chance of winning. Few people are talented enough to carry a team or business on their shoulders. They are a rarity. Wilt was one of them.

I was just the opposite. For me to guarantee victory, I had to give to my teammates. My goal was to keep them doing their best so I could be at mine. When a ball reached me in the mid-dle, it was as though my eyesight and my hands got better. I could see from sideline to sideline, knowing where each of my teammates was. My impulse was to get the ball to someone who was in a position to shoot. More and more, I prided myself on my passing. I never made fancy passes, but I always made good ones that allowed my teammates to catch the ball and usually to find themselves in a spot where they were open to shoot it. Plays went through me. I could pass or set a pick for a teammate, turning my body, my hip, in just the right way to free up a teammate for a drive to the basket or for an open jumper. On defense, my goal was to intimidate opponents—as a way of sparking my team. A rebound was the first step of the offense. When I blocked a shot, I'd sometimes, in the same motion, direct it to a teammate starting up the floor the other way. If a player got me up in the air and went past me, I learned how to recover and block his shot from behind or to block two or three shots in one sequence—all of this with the sense that my team would be lifted. That lifted me.

> *I learned something essential in my ego battles with Wilt. Ego is not a principle so much as a force of energy in the self. It is the vital current in your body, what you bring to everything you do, it is the power in you that can create positive (or negative) results in your life. No matter what the job or station you find yourself in, ego is the force of energy you summon that will allow you to be fully present and engaged. If energy is misdirected or is absent, success will be impossible.*

I want to make one thing clear: ego is about using yourself to your own best advantage, getting the most out of yourself and your abilities, but only in the context of your team's ability to win. That is often not easy to see. I know someone who is the CEO of a Fortune 500 company. This man worked in a business for twenty-five years, trying as hard as he could to advance. He reached a certain level and could go no further because the business was family-owned and all the top-level executive positions were held by family members. He knew what he wanted, understood his abilities and what they might bring to his life and to those people he worked for and served. But it took him twenty-five years before he finally quit his job, went out and raised money, and started his own company. Then, after he was able to do that, he turned around and bought the company he had worked for—not out of any sense of revenge but because he understood why his leadership in that company was so necessary—to him and to that business. His ego demanded that—and it directly benefited his business and those who worked for him.

My Celtic teammate Sam Jones was an example of ego operating in still another and more subtle way. Sam could literally do anything he wanted on a basketball court. He had the ability to take over any team he played for, including the Boston Celtics. If he had wanted, he might have wound up as the NBA's all-time scoring champion. But that's not what he wanted. "Sam, don't you know how good you are?" I asked him one time. "Yeah," he said, "but I just don't want that kind of responsibility." In some ways, Sam always kept me wondering, but I knew he was as committed to our success as anyone else. One time, we were down two games to one in a five-game semifinal play-off against Cincinnati. Game four was on their court. Before the game, Sam came to me and told me he needed me to carry the load that night, but that if I did, he would guarantee game five for us. We beat the Royals that night. I had a really big game, and we tied the series. When we came out for the final game at Boston Garden, Sam, as he took his place in line during the introductions, turned to me and winked. He then proceeded to score forty-seven points.

Sam had a great understanding of his ego. For him to do his best, to produce the results that would be best for him and his team, he had to drop back and let others take over. He was always ready to step in and take over when that was called for, but that was not ever his goal. Sam didn't want the day-to-day pressures of being a superstar. The knowledge he had of himself guided him to create exactly the results that were most fulfilling to him. His ego demanded this, and the results were beneficial to him and to everyone who played with him. If he had ever let others dictate to him what he needed to be, he would never have been the great player he really was. His superb gifts would have gone for naught if he had tried to twist them into the makeup of a personality he did not have.

Let's review a few of Russell's Rules for building team ego as these can be applied to all aspects of life:

RUSSELL RULES

Rule One: Establish your business environment. Help everyone understand the power in decision-making that benefits the team.

Rule Two: Make sure the team is part of the process. Help your business team or family or basketball team understand not only what's going to happen but also the whys and the hows.

Rule Three: Create unselfishness as the most important team attribute. Philip Caldwell, the former CEO at Ford who helped turn the company around, made many memorable statements. One that impressed me was "The important thing to recognize is that it takes a team. And the team ought to get credit for both the wins and the losses. Successes have many fathers, failures none."

Sometime after I quit playing, the Celtics wanted to retire my number. Red called me and asked me if I would take part in a ceremony at the Garden where my jersey would be raised to the rafters. I turned him down saying that was not important to me. He replied, "But you have to." So he asked again and I said no again. He kept asking and I kept turning him down. Then, one time, when I was in Boston to cover a game, he brought it up once more. I took the same position. You can retire my number, I said, but I wasn't going to be around to watch it. Red accused me of being stubborn and willful—which he knew I was anyway—and wanted to know why, why I wanted to shun such an honor from the fans. Because I never played for the fans, I explained, I played for myself and for my team. I told Red I felt honored to have my number retired but that was something I could in good conscience only do with my team-mates. Everything I had done I had done with them and with no one else. So what Red then proposed was that the ceremony take place before the game that night—prior to the time when fans were admitted to the building—with only my teammates and him in attendance. That I gladly agreed to.

Later, when word got out about what had happened, one of my many critics took pains to point out that what I had done was a colossal act of egotism. I had chosen to show to the world—and the Boston Celtics—the size of my own ego.

He was exactly right. Except for the fact that my ego was always about my team.

LISTENING IS
NEVER CASUAL

LISTENING IS ESSENTIAL TO WINNING. THERE IS NO WAY around it. If you do not listen, you cannot win. Poor listening habits get in the way of success in both personal and professional relationships. The most important thing any business leader needs to know about listening is that there is a difference between hearing and listening. I remember that, when I was a freshman at the University of San Francisco, I went into the recreation room and a bunch of older guys were there working out.

One of the bigger guys turned and said to me, "You're a tall one."

I didn't respond.

Then he said, "What's your name, freshman?"

I said, "My name is William."

"Hmmm," he said. "I am going to give you a nickname." A few minutes later he came back and said, "I am going to call you ———" (it was very disparaging, so I am not going to repeat it here).

"You'd better not," I said in response. "And if you do, I am going to whack you."

I thought I had made my point. But a half hour later, he walked by me on his way out of the rec room and said to me, "See ya, ———."

The next thing he said was "Why did you do that?"

As he picked himself up off the floor, I said, "Weren't you listening to me?"

Maybe we are not teaching our children how to listen because it seems to me that eighty percent of people hear while only twenty percent really listen. If this were an illness (and I do believe it is catching), it could be considered an epidemic. One of the consequences of a society that can't or just won't listen is a shallowness of understanding and no appreciation for anything but the simpleminded. I have great frustration with our society on this issue. The failure to listen or understand how to listen has contributed to our society's hurtling through relationships as if one had just bought a book and breezed through it looking only at the pictures. The success of publications like USA Today certainly validates this hypothesis in my mind.

In the middle of my playing career, I decided to stop signing autographs. In part, my feeling about autographs is based upon by my belief that I'd rather meet someone who approaches me respectfully, talk to them for a minute and look them in the eye, rather than participate in the momentary ritual of signing something, never looking at the person I'm signing something for, never getting to know them, and then moving on.

Perhaps because we had no formal listening training in grade school and all of us can hear, we assume we are listening when we really aren't. We can be in the middle of an intense conversation with someone and our mind can be a million miles away. Imagine the consequences of that sort of thing when it comes to decision-making, or to things you absolutely need to know about your business or family. We have one tongue and two ears because listening is that important. Lee Iacocca said, "Listening is the single skill that makes the difference between a mediocre and a great company."

At this point, you may be asking how you can develop or foster in yourself and the people around you, whether it be business associates, teammates, or friends and family members, the skill of listening.

I give you Russell's Three Rules for Becoming an Effective Listener:

RUSSELL RULES

Rule One: Listening is more important than talking. When you are an active listener, you are respecting what the other person is feeling or expressing.

Rule Two: Listening is a skill that requires you to subordinate your own views when listening to someone else. The more you practice the more you will be able to distinguish, for yourself, the difference between hearing and listening. Start by keeping the mouth tightly closed. I do not mean to be cute, but if you have grown up in the type of family where dinner conversations are laced with noisy interruptions, this may be tough, but don't give up. The point is that to become an effective listener you may have to break some bad habits.

Rule Three: Convert your listening skills to effective language skills. Once you have learned to listen, become especially mindful of the kinds of words and phrases you use that will help others listen to you more effectively. Listening is ultimately about effective communication, and everyone can benefit from that. The effort and practice of effective listening has a big payoff in every facet of life. I've noticed time and again that we as humans tend to respect and even to like those who listen to us even if they disagree with us. It is a basic but powerful human need to be understood, and the effective listener is filling that need as well as gaining information that he or she may need.

So, someone who listens obviously has many advantages that others do not have, among them: being able to discriminate between what someone says and what he or she really means; being able to absorb necessary information in making decisions; being able to act and interact in a positive and empowering way with others. In all my years as an active listener, I have noticed six bad habits that people fall into when they are hearing but not listening. Take a look at the following list and see how many you answer with a yes.

1. Do you find yourself trying to come up with a "better" story than the one the speaker is telling?
2. Are you nodding yes when you are not really listening just to keep the conversation moving?
3. Do you make eye contact with the speaker?
4. Do you find that you forget what has been said immediately following the conversation?

5. Are you asking trivial questions to seem as if you are listening?

6. Are you always interrupting because you feel you have a "more important" thing to say?

It surprises me still that people take in only what they want to hear. I remember when I ended my career as a player. I was doing commentary for ABC during a play-off series between the Knicks and the Lakers. After the series was over, I got letters from many people. In one of these letters, a fan from Indiana wanted to know why I hated the Lakers. Los Angeles, he told me, played great, were a cohesive team, played clean basketball, and were the epitome of what a championship team should be. I opened another letter from a fan in New Jersey wanting to know why I hated the Knicks. He used almost the same language. I was so struck by this that I mailed the letter from the Indiana fan to the guy from New Jersey, and the New Jersey letter to the guy from Indiana. Those letters made me understand that oftentimes the prejudice of the listener, including opinions, distorts the message so much that it is almost unrecognizable in terms of what was actually said. For some,

> **When a team is functioning on all cylinders, listening is an essential component of success. A team, whether it's a sports team, a business, or a family, cannot function effectively unless you and everyone else are prepared to drop the filters that get in the way of effective listening.**

zipping the lip is just the beginning. There may also be the need to still your mind while someone is speaking, especially if you have strong feelings about the topic of conversation.

In corporate life, good team listening skills are a must. How can a company consisting of many divisions and operating on a budget of millions or billions expect to do well unless there is planning, cooperation, coordination at all levels. Take a corporation like Costco, for example, a company I am familiar with because I know the CEO reasonably well. The company now has nearly three hundred different outlets worldwide and is still growing. Anytime you walk into any one of the stores, it is obvious things are running well from top to bottom. Service is always efficient and courteous, the stores are immaculate, business is brisk, there are never any problems with inventory. The proof of the operation is not only in the company's profitability, but in the atmosphere of cooperation that is apparent in any Costco outlet. Whenever my friend visits one of his stores, his employees know who he is right away. Everyone is on a first-name basis, each member of the company knows he or she can approach the boss because he has made it a principle of management to encourage listening. People who work for him know that what they say will be heard—and may well be acted upon. The same is true in many other well-run, high-powered businesses. Leadership involves listening as much as it does setting policy. In fact, in a well-run company, large or small, sound policy decisions depend on listening.

That's what I found when I finally got to the Celtics. Because each of us players was a star in his own right, the only way we could have been effective was by the ability we all developed to work with each other. Listening made it easier for us to be friends, but most of all it enabled us to do our job, to win games and championships.

When I think of Red Auerbach and the leadership he provided, I think of someone who not only had a supreme basketball mind but a great set of ears. Red's greatest talent was that he was a listener who translated what he heard into effective action. How did he do it?

Red was the first coach who coached me personally. No matter how good you are you need someone to bounce ideas off of and push back some new thoughts. Because if you don't, that groove can very quickly become a rut. Every now and then Red would call me to come to a game or practice early and we'd just talk. He might say, you're getting a little off track. And the conversations were always useful because he used a language that I could hear.

He spoke to each of us differently. This was never an affectation. He had an uncanny ability to pick up intonations, inflections, and body language in every one of his players. When he listened, he had what I like to think of as a built-in, shockproof lie detector. We used to have a saying on the Celtics, "Don't lie to me, boy!" That came from Red. He insisted that players tell him exactly what was on their mind. That meant spelling out in the clearest possible basketball terms what they could and couldn't do on the court. He wanted straight answers so he could make good decisions. And he knew how to solicit those answers, and he had the wiliest instinct for eliminating the difficult space between someone's words and their intentions.

The key to Red's method was that when he asked a question or wanted to know if you could do something, he did it in such a way that you knew you had room to answer him without feeling threatened. In itself that was an enormous boon to a player who might have felt he could not speak his mind for fear of job security. But that wasn't the end of it. If you did say no to Red, he would want to know why. Again there was no threat in the question. It was clear to the player that what Red was after was accurate information. Then, and only if Red was able to hear something in that player's answer, would he suggest that there might be a way to teach you or to do something a little differently. The player, for his part, would be expected to hear that and integrate it—again with no sense of penalty hanging over his head.

In the specific ways Red adapted himself to different players, he had to take into account who they were. With Cousy, for example, Red welcomed rather than resented that Cousy walked, talked, and thought like a captain of a team. Red never told Cousy he had to do this or do that, which would have made him feel like a corporal. Red would always ask him questions, seeking his advice. "Cooz, what do you think we need in this situation? Do you want to run twenty or twenty-one? Or do you want do something else?" Cousy would mull it over and then spell out why he preferred one play over another until both men understood they had come up with the right answer. Because of the enormous respect everyone had for Cousy, Red knew the rest of us would never feel slighted by this "negotiating" process.

Red handled Tommy Heinsohn completely differently. He was a rough-and-ready player who despite his proclivity for temper tantrums was, and is, one of my most favorite teammates. Red talked to Tommy the way Tommy would talk, because Red knew Tommy would listen more effectively. Red always wanted Heinsohn to work on his physical conditioning. He knew Tommy wasn't in the best shape he could be. But Tommy wouldn't acknowledge that. In one game when Heinsohn hit something like eight straight shots, Red pulled him out. Tommy had smoke coming out of his ears. Red said, "I'm taking you out because if you're working as hard as you're supposed to be, you've got to be tired, and if you're not tired, you should be!" It was stunning. What Red had done was find a way to catch Tommy's ear, to make him listen. If Red had pulled him at a time when Tommy wasn't going well, when his shots weren't falling or his man was beating him on the other end, Tommy would never have assumed his coming out of the game had anything to do with his being out of shape. Not so in this case. Red had found a dramatic and clever way to get his attention.

Red had a harder time with Bill Sharman, who wasn't at all boisterous but who was extremely stubborn. Sharman had his way of doing things and it didn't always mesh with what Red wanted. Red believed, for example—as an article of faith— that if a player was open and had a choice, his best shot would always be closer to the basket, preferably a layup. Sharman, on the other hand, wanted to take jump shots because he didn't believe his skills were best used going to the basket. Because Sharman was so hard-nosed, there was just no way he was vulnerable to any of Red's devices—and Red knew that. They had a conflict of viewpoints—something that can also happen on good teams—and each man chose to leave it at that rather than push the other. It took unusual listening skills in both of them to preserve the peace. Neither man was willing to confront the other. Red listened to Sharman and backed off.

Sharman listened to Red and did what he could to accommodate him without ever changing his basic game.

Red was a great leader because of the trust and respect he had earned among his players. It had everything to do with listening. In 1963, when we were going for a fifth straight NBA title, he turned up at a practice with his usual big pack of cigars and with a new play he boldly stated would be the key to our next championship. He got all of us together, diagrammed his great new play, then had us run it for the next hour and a half. Then he called us together again and you could see how pleased he was. With his chest stuck out and his hands on his hips, you could almost feel the electricity leaping from him.

"Well, Cooz, whaddaya think?" he asked.

Cousy shrugged. "I think it's a piece of crap, Red." There was dead silence in the gym.

Then Red turned to Sharman, who told him the same thing—but a little more politely: "Well, Red, if you go here with this guy and there with that guy, then you've got no one to slide over and cover here. The whole play breaks down, it's just a waste of time."

Now the silence in the place was thick as a blanket.

Red turned to me. "How 'bout you, Russ?"

"Those are the two most articulate guys on the club, Red. I can't say it any better!"

Now Red could have imposed the play on us, insisted we run it because he knew it would really work, but instead we never heard about it again. And he never took it back to the drawing board to rework it that season or in any season following. Red listened, and when he heard the team unite in their opposition, he didn't fight it. He let it go.

> *When listening is most productive, it is always about communication. It is two-sided even when one person is left to make a decision. It takes into account the words, the viewpoints, of others and then respects them. To be a good listener it is imperative that you become free enough of your own agenda to really hear someone else.*

In 1973 when my first marriage had ended and I asked for and got custody of my eleven-year-old daughter, I had to hone my listening skills to be a more effective parent. Parenting is tough, and learning to listen to your kids is probably the toughest part of it. But I knew I had to communicate with her and that I knew nothing about eleven-year-old girls. So to help me listen and learn and find a common ground for us to share a common interest, I hit on this idea of her reading the newspaper every day, choosing a story, and then she and I discussing it at breakfast. It became a forum to listen to each other about current events. But it wasn't ever about sports. The newspaper stories were just a way of helping me listen, to get my daughter talking to me so that I could begin to know what was on her mind.

We're all bilingual. Most people, for example, are called on to use different languages for different audiences. We all have both public and private languages. For example, when you are going to a business meeting, you have to adjust your language to allow your audiences to listen to you more effectively. You need to choose words that are more than idioms or clichés for your industry because many people tend to hear those all-too-familiar words and tune out. Choose words that cause people to think, "What does he mean by that?" When I speak to audiences, I always try to use words that they might not expect, words they do not always hear, so I know they are listening to the point I am trying to make. But you would not use this technique with your family. At home, developing an inviting language encourages honesty, dialogue, and sharing of feelings that will prove to deliver a much more enriching relationship with your family.

> *I learned a great deal from the Jesuits at the University of San Francisco. Not only did the priests teach us about the importance of making distinctions, they used to tell us over and over again that we had to learn how to distinguish true from false statements. Their method was simple. After defining the terms, you had to consider the source.*

What a useful tool this has become for me. It was so much easier for me to evaluate outside opinions and judgments when I asked myself those two basic questions: What is really being said and who is saying it? To illustrate the practical way this worked in my life, I want to take you back to that first year in Boston again.

Bob Cousy, at that point, was the most revered player on the Celtics, a Boston icon. To me, from the start, Cousy, as I've said before, was all I could ever want for a teammate. He was the one who first embraced me on the team, he was the one who took it on himself to make sure I would be a part of that team. But one day, after I had been with the team for a while, a really prominent Boston writer came up to me wanting to know what Cousy had taught me. "Nothing," I said. The writer got mad. "Whaddaya mean nothing?" he said. I told him again, Cousy didn't teach me anything. Was I saying, the writer wanted to know, that I couldn't learn anything from so great a player?

Bob Cousy was surely a great player, I said, and I am the best center anywhere. But while he could teach me about playing guard, he certainly couldn't teach me a thing about playing center. You can imagine the story that followed. I was arrogant, self-centered, unappreciative, and insanely jealous of Cousy. The writer's story did not mean anything to me because the conclusion was wrong, and so was the motivation for writing it. It had no value.

I considered the source of the story. He was a writer looking for a headline. And then I considered the definitions. The writer, perhaps without understanding it himself, was using terms that had to do with playing guard—not center. The writer assumed that the term *great player* was useful in itself. It was not. I was able to listen to myself and know that what I was hearing was reliable. The information I was providing myself was useful for me, but also for my team.

So, let's take a twenty-second time-out to sum up. Listening is a leadership skill that has to be developed. It is about respecting others and yourself enough so that you can put yourself, your company, your family, in position to win. The Russell Rules for listening are clear:

RUSSELL RULES

Rule One: Make sure your ears are open enough not only to catch what is said, but to pick up the intention of the speaker.

Rule Two: Make sure you know your own intention as a listener. Are you hearing, or are you listening?

Rule Three: This is the most important of the rules: Combine these very different intentions that you pick up from listening into something that can help you make useful decisions. Call it translation, call it interaction, but what is most essential is having an ability to combine what is said with what is meant so that useful decision-making may follow.

Let's make sure in applying the rules that we accept the idea that there are honest differences between people. Sometimes choosing not to act is the best thing you can do for the sake of the proper functioning of the team.

> *Above all, keep in mind Russell's Corollary to the Three Rules of Listening: Always make sure you are able to listen to yourself to the point where you know that what you are picking up is the voice of wisdom.*

TOUGHNESS OR TENDERNESS: CREATING YOUR LEADERSHIP STYLE

I DO NOT BELIEVE LEADERS ARE BORN LEADERS. LEADERSHIP IS an acquired skill. And, most important, leadership, like swimming, has to be learned through active participation and practice. It cannot be learned solely through observation. Great leaders in my opinion possess three flexible skills: toughness, tenderness, and the ability to know when is the right time to use one or the other. This is one of the most valuable skills any leader can gain.

I remember reading an article about researchers who were trying to find the traits that serve as predictors of future leaders. Height, as I recall, was one of those traits. But Napoleon Bonaparte certainly contradicts that theory. In the end, after years of study, the researchers could only conclude that different leadership styles were necessary for different circumstances, and that the most successful leaders could change styles as the needs of the company, team, or family changed.

The choice of how to lead is more than a skill. It is a reflection of both the leader himself and of the culture he or she has created for the company. I once told an audience of corporate salespeople how impressed I was with Tom May from Nstar in Boston. NStar is Massachusetts's largest investor-owned electrical gas utility. He could get anything out of his colleagues because he could relate to them. Every problem, every project, every change, was shaped into a metaphor, an analogy, or expressed as a picture. He'd never say, "I want this done!" It would always be "I wonder if we can do that." or "I think it could look more like this." And then he would begin exploring the problem, project, or plan with his employees.

So how does Tom May's vision of leadership fit into Russell's Rules? Here are some basic rules for leadership style:

RUSSELL RULES

Rule One: Successful teams of any kind are benevolent dictatorships. If you lead wisely, you'll be followed cheerfully.

Rule Two: Be adaptable. Great leaders can follow as well as lead. It's the difference between an outside-in leader and an inside-out leader. Outside-in leaders are always finding ways to include others, to use, draw out, and promote others in their counsels and decision-making. Inside-out leaders rely solely on their own intuition, logic, and counsel, which they then project outward in the form of commands.

Rule Three: Real kindness is an act of strength and a tremendous leadership asset. Two thoughts my grandfather left me with were to praise loudly and blame softly, and not to forget a throne is nothing more than a bench covered in velvet.

As I mentioned, I now find myself speaking regularly to groups and companies on leadership and winning. At one of these meetings, a CEO came up to me and said, "You're so right about being outside-in versus inside-out. Here is the way I've tried to get my company to look at leadership. It's by remembering the important concepts in terms of employee-driven phrases." I so liked what the CEO had to say about outside-in management that I will repeat it here. It goes like this:

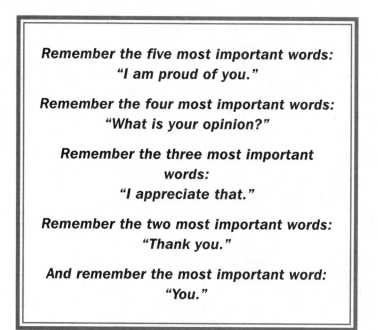

> **Remember the five most important words:**
> **"I am proud of you."**
>
> **Remember the four most important words:**
> **"What is your opinion?"**
>
> **Remember the three most important words:**
> **"I appreciate that."**
>
> **Remember the two most important words:**
> **"Thank you."**
>
> **And remember the most important word:**
> **"You."**

One time, on my very first day as player-coach of the Celtics, when all the guys knew me as just another teammate, I went to my locker before practice and discovered that my shoes were missing. The guys, as a prank, had stolen them. I asked "politely" where they were. Hiding their smiles, nobody volunteered to tell me where they were. After the team had gone out to the gym, one of the trainers and I searched around until we finally found the shoes. I took them and locked them away somewhere else. Then I went out and told my players we were going to run all day unless my shoes were returned. I told them I wasn't interested in learning the identity of the thief, but I had to have my shoes back. With that I excused myself and said I'd be back in fifteen minutes and that I fully expected my shoes to be there by then.

My teammates, not wanting to run all day, decided to return them—except that when they went to get them, they were gone. When I returned to the gym, the shoes were still missing. This time they weren't smiling as much. And started running. As much as I wanted to join them, I couldn't because I didn't have any shoes. Wayne Embry said he lost twenty-five pounds that day; other guys were wheezing and holding their sides. I did what I had to do to establish my authority as coach. I could not be just another one of the guys, as enjoyable as that had always been for me. My job, like it or not, was to be the team's coach and to make sure there was no doubt about that. At the same time, it was important for me not to separate myself from my teammates. I ran with them in my stocking feet. I exerted myself as much as any of them. I made sure that the "punishment" was not a punishment but an afternoon of hard conditioning—a basic staple of life on the Boston Celtics— something that in the end was beneficial to us all.

I knew there was no maliciousness in the prank my teammates had pulled. We all liked each other, had all spent years horsing around together like brothers in a family. It didn't matter. It was necessary for all of us to understand that there was a new relationship between us and that it was necessary if the Celtics were to have continued success.

The first principle of developing a leadership style of any kind, as I see it, is toughness. Of all the characteristics of leaders this is the one that is most easily misunderstood and the one that is most necessary. Some very unlikely people— Mother Teresa, Gandhi, Martin Luther King Jr.—exemplify toughness. These people were not tyrants or intimidators, as one would expect a person exhibiting toughness would be. But they had convictions and beliefs that they held on to with fierce determination. That is an outward sign of toughness.

> **Toughness is the ability to shut out all that is irrelevant in reaching a goal and to inspire others to follow you.**

Some folks misconstrue toughness and fear. Fear is never inspirational, although it has the power to achieve results. You do not lead by hitting people over the head . . . that is assault, not leadership. Dictators who rely on fear as a motivation talk about toughness, but don't have it or understand it. Here is another cardinal rule for understanding and using toughness in your leadership style:

> **A good leader is always a follower as much as he is a ruler. The team comes first. That was why Red listened to his players and got out of the way when he felt they were right.**

Toughness is a shield that is surprisingly supple, flexible, and resilient. It protects you so that you can be a real team player—or leader—allowing you to accept demands that may not always be pleasant but that are necessary for success. I never liked fighting, for example. But I learned that on certain occasions I would have to do it or fail at what I most wanted for myself. I have always tried to avoid fighting, knowing that it was a stupid way to prove yourself. But if I had to defend myself, I did.

When I was at USF, we played against Holy Cross. We were a championship team at that point and developing a fearsome reputation for our commitment to winning. As we warmed up before the game with our layup drills, the Holy Cross players were totally distressed. As the first ball went into play, I could see they were totally intimidated. The only player who was not intimidated was Tommy Heinsohn. He kept fruitlessly exhorting his teammates, "Don't be afraid of Russell! Don't be afraid of him!" In the middle of the second quarter we were walking back up the court to line up for a foul shot when he took one step ahead of me and planted his elbow right in the middle of my stomach as hard as he could. Yes, it hurt! I showed no reaction, didn't say anything, and just kept walking. Perhaps a little hunched over. I waited about five or six minutes. I called for the ball from the pivot position. K.C. threw it to me and I immediately passed it across court knowing that everyone from the referees to the fans would be watching the flight of the ball. I recoiled and planted the hardest elbow ever in the middle of Tommy's stomach. I can't even describe the sound he made; all I know is that he collapsed. I just walked away. At that point everyone turned and saw him stretched out. And to this day, he and I were the only people who knew what happened.

In the thirteen years I was a player, I think had three or four fights, none that I ever sought, but all of them ones where I felt I had no choice but to respond, where walking away would have created more problems for me than if I'd fought. Fighting was not how I showed toughness. Doing what was necessary to stand up for myself was.

The most interesting challenge I had as a leader was when I became coach and general manager of the Seattle Super-Sonics in 1973. The year before, the Sonics had won only twenty-six games and were indisputably one of the worst teams and organizations in the league. One afternoon when I was handling phone calls on a drive-time talk show in L.A., Sam Schulman, owner of Sonics, a guy who had a reputation for devouring coaches as quickly as he hired them, called in and asked me to call him back after I got off the air. I did and he said he was again dissatisfied with his coach and asked if I had anyone I would recommend. I recommended five different guys. He said none of them met his qualifications.

He called back about a week later and said, "Why don't you take the job?"

I told him I wasn't interested.

"Why?" he asked.

"I am not interested," I answered truthfully, "and besides, no one wants to work for you."

"What do you mean?"

"Well, you are always interfering and you just don't let your coaches succeed."

"I don't interfere," he replied a little defensively.

"Sam, we like each other, let's not go there. But that's why you have a new coach every year." I had clearly given him something to think about because he cut the conversation off at that point.

He waited another couple of weeks and called again. This time he said, "What would it take for you to take the job?"

I told him what it would take: a lot of money and absolute control of the franchise and team. But control was more important than the money. I would have to be the general manager, too.

"Why do you need all that?"

"Because I am not coming to Seattle to put my name and reputation on the line without that leadership responsibility." I had put my demands on the table for Sam. I believe that no team is any better than its front office. It doesn't make a difference how much money they give you if you don't have the tools to do the job.

To my amazement Sam went along with my demands—and so then, for the first time, I thought seriously about whether I wanted the job. In the end, I took it because I was curious to see how well I could do with this new challenge.

Seattle was suffering from the same things that many young franchises suffer from. They were trying to create a brand without assets, reputation, and performance history. By bringing me into the organization, Sam was gaining instant credibility.

When I took over, the average nightly attendance at Sonics games was something like forty-six hundred—and not growing. We didn't have a very good team, for a number of reasons. First, they had no team ego. Petty egos were rampant. There was no sense of loyalty. No sense of tradition. And no one had really given them insights into how to win. There were few friendships on the team, and the couple of guys who did hang out with each other did so as a way of supporting their own negative attitudes about the team, the city, and the management.

I wanted to do everything I could to get this group together. The first thing I did was to devise a plan for success. The plan was simple: use plays that required every player on the floor to be doing something in coordination. I brought in the Celtics' system-five "simple" plays—not because I didn't know anything else, but because I knew those plays could only work if everyone was pulling together. Other, more complicated systems around the league were built around individual stars. But I knew winning would only come from creating a team, and this system was the best way to do that.

My management style embraced toughness. It achieved the desired result quickly, producing respect, attention, and team commitment. Toughness in this scenario focused my team on their own capability for commitment. Had I chosen an alternative management style, I am convinced they just wouldn't have listened, responded, or come together. I ran hard practices just the way Red had. The goal of the practices had nothing to do with the hours spent but with what was accomplished. Conditioning was crucial, but so was running plays and getting the players to understand that I wanted them to become their own best teachers rather than relying on me. If the plays were run correctly, with all the subtle variations that were in them, the players would have to use all their creativity and individual skills to the maximum. If they did not, they would fail. It was as simple as that. Nurturing is important, but first everyone has to be listening. My team knew what I stood for . . . but they also knew what I wouldn't stand for.

A word about hard practices. A friend of mine once bragged that he hit three hundred golf balls in one session. I told him that that was a remarkable number, but I asked him, did he learn anything? If you hit three hundred or five hundred balls and you understand something about your swing you didn't understand before, that's just right. If you hit one thousand balls, turn your hands into raw blisters, but learn nothing, then it is all a waste of time. The test is being able at the end of that hard practice to put ten or fifteen balls within a foot of each other.

That, in effect, was what I was trying for with the SuperSonics.

When practices didn't go well, when I saw that players were either putting in hours or just playing for themselves, I had them run laps as a team. I made personnel decisions that didn't sit well. The harshest form of discipline in my industry is to deprive a player of playing time. A lot of my players found themselves sitting more than they wanted.

There was one player (let's keep him nameless) who reacted so sharply to what he felt was his diminished playing time that he physically threatened me one evening in the locker room. He walked up to me, with his teammates standing around, and said flat out that he wasn't getting enough time and that he didn't like the way I was running the team. I didn't say a word. I just looked at the guy. I knew that he had physically threatened the last coach of the team, so this wasn't a total surprise. My silence provoked him even more. "I'm gonna have to kick your butt!" he finally shouted at me. I said then that if that's what he had to do, so be it. I didn't really know what was in his mind, but the matter stalled right there. His teammates walked him away, we went out and played our game, and I used this player in exactly the way I had been using him. However, the matter between us was far from over.

Some weeks later, he came into my office and said he was going to shoot me. Maybe because I came from West Oakland, I didn't feel intimidated. That's interesting, I told him, and then gave him some information. I pointed out that the gun he was going to shoot me with had most likely been mass-produced and the chances were that several hundred or thousand of them had been manufactured that same day, and that gun shops sold guns to anybody who wanted them, and that it was just a logical assumption that many people, including those whose lives were threatened, might be gun owners, too. Think of it this way, I said: You go hunting for deer and to your surprise you find that the deer have guns. Do you know what that means? That means you're going to be in the middle of a war, not a hunt.

I'm still here to talk about that episode so I know it worked on one level, but the job of building the Sonics into a real team continued. I had to convey that I cared for my team, my players, our mutual success, as much as I did about any willingness I had to use my authority.

In my first year as head coach, the Sonics won ten more games than they had the previous season when they won only twenty-six. The second year, we missed winning the Pacific Division by five games and went to the second round of the play-offs, the first time the Sonics had ever been in postseason. Ultimately, the Sonics won an NBA Championship with the foundation and team I had put together.

> *For me, the example of how a diversified management style succeeds will always be the Boston Celtics. The Celtics practiced a benevolent despotism. It was easy to play for them, the work was hard, the rewards were almost infinite. There was a joy of playing and of belonging to this team. It is impossible to talk about the Celtics without coming to grips with this different notion of toughness.*

The owner of the Celtics was Walter Brown, one of the most decent men who ever lived and someone who was completely, totally, irreversibly dedicated to bringing championships to Boston. He was as tough as Red Auerbach was.

Everything Walter did came from his heart. Year after year, he kept pouring money into the Celtics and would have gone bankrupt before he ever considered giving up the team. Among NBA owners, he was always considered fair and honest to a fault. Red used to roll his eyes when Walter talked about "the good of the league" because Red was scared silly that Walter's good nature would somehow get in the way. As a benevolent dictator, Walter's way of handling this "defect" in his nature was to turn the running of the team completely over to Red.

Once, some big-shot oil executive from Texas who knew Walter collared him and told him he had found one of the great basketball players in America and would Walter please allow the player to try out for the Celtics. Now this was totally out of line; there were no "tryouts" for amateurs on the Celtics. Nevertheless Walter persuaded Red to let the player have a shot.

When we got to practice that day, Red told us in this strangely mumbling voice that Walter, as a favor, wanted this new guy to work out with the team, that he had been assured the guy was a great player. The oilman had told Red the guy was better than Bob Cousy and that we should just go out and work hard and do what we had to do. Red was expecting to see us grind the guy into hamburger.

Well, the first time the player got his hands on the ball, he made an obvious head fake and Cousy fell down. The guy drove to the basket and scored. Next time, same thing. When Sharman covered him, he wound up on the floor. When the guy got loose and came toward the basket, I stepped out of the way. Tommy and K.C., everyone, just stood there or moved a step too slowly while the oilman's kid went wild. It took Red

> **What has to be understood about toughness is that it is necessary only because a team, a business, a family, cannot exist without core leadership. Decisions can be made in many ways, top-down or democratically, but ultimately there must be responsibility for decision-making.**

the better part of the afternoon before he finally caught on and cut the guy.

In corporate life, the nature of the dictator, benevolent or otherwise, will determine just how well or poorly a company does. The success of a dictator of course ultimately depends on the bottom line, but the most essential aspect has to do with leadership and management style. The leadership is there to establish a brand people can believe in and not just a profit. The bottom line will ultimately vary from year to year, but the brand must remain firmly fixed in the mind of the public. Think about IBM, General Motors, and Johnson & Johnson in recent years. They all have had their ups and downs, but the brands they control represent organizations with established core leaderships. The team on the field is always there to support the brands, not the needs of anyone's individual whims. That creates a consistent winning effort, and that is why Big Blue, Ford pickup trucks, and Band-Aids remain in the forefront of consumers' minds year in and year out.

Red Auerbach was also a great, tender dictator. He was the best basketball mind I have ever encountered, the hardest taskmaster, the easiest coach in the world to play for, the one who, more than any other, accomplished success through respecting his players, bullying them, inspiring them, always being on their side even when he seemed to be standing over them with a whip. And it was always for the Celtics.

Once, prior to the time when back surgery produced consistently positive results, Jim Loscutoff, a burly forward on our team, was coming back from a severe injury. Red knew that Loscutoff was unsure if he would ever be able to play again. Red devised a little game for him in practice called fetch. Red stood at the foul circle and had Losky stand off around fifteen feet away. Red tried to bounce balls past him on either side and had him dive to stop them, burning dozens of "strawberries" onto his elbows and knees. Finally, at about the point when Loscutoff was scraped raw, Red said, "Well, if you can do that, you surely can play!" and walked away. Loscutoff was in a rage; he told all of us that when he retired, he intended to kill Red. And he never forgot. Following his last game, he asked all of us to leave him alone with Red for two minutes so he could finally confront him man to man about that incident. We did. But we lingered nearby just in case things got out of hand. When we heard noise that sounded a little out of the ordinary, we quickly stepped in, but instead of finding Losky all over Red, we found him sitting there with tears streaming down his cheeks telling Red how much he loved him and how much Red had done for him over the years. Loscutoff knew, as we all did, that everything Red did was for his team and hence for all of us.

I want to make sure I am understood when I discuss tenderness because it is usually not thought of as a leadership trait,

> *Tenderness is always the result of intelligence. In other words, tenderness allowed these leaders to better see and respect the talents of those they were dealing with. Far from being soft-headed, these leaders were exhibiting farsightedness that led directly to the enormous successes they achieved in life. A tyrant without tenderness, a tough guy who prides himself on his toughness, may accomplish things, but does so with a reluctant army behind him.*

and yet in my mind it is one of the most potent of powers. As I see it, leaders like Walter Brown and Red Auerbach were infinitely more effective because they had this unexpected side to them. But why tenderness should be effective rather than merely decorative is interesting.

A few potent Russell Rules to sum up why toughness and tenderness are the opposable skills that every winner needs to manage in nearly every aspect of his life:

RUSSELL RULES

Rule One: Successful teams of any kind are dictatorships. This is not a bad thing, but a necessary component of a winning team.

Rule Two: Good dictators follow as well as lead. They will encourage, not discourage, the people who work for them.

Rule Three: Tenderness is an act of strength and can be a most powerful leadership trait when it is used to recognize and promote the abilities and talents of others.

INVISIBLE MAN

INVISIBILITY IS USUALLY NOT A STANDARD BY WHICH ANYONE measures success, but it is a great power if it is understood and used creatively. It is a subtle power. It resists formulas and definitions, but its rewards are extraordinary.

Most people think of invisibility as a trait of superheroes or the basis for early science-fiction movies. There's an old movie, called *The Invisible Man*, where the hero is chased by a mob who want to kill him. The guy is wearing a suit of clothes and his head is swathed in bandages so he can go out on the street. But when the mob decides to lynch him and then closes in on him, he strips naked, unwinds the bandages from his head, and easily slips away. There's an old crime-fighting radio hero called the Shadow, who used the power of his invisibility to preserve, protect, and defend the common good. That is all well and good for fiction, but can invisibility become a staple of your leadership style and help you become a winner? Absolutely.

Because invisibility flies in the face of our culture where only what can be seen is considered real, where we base our day-to-day lives on our five senses, we just don't think much about what's invisible or about that power we have to make ourselves unseen. But this can be a most potent tool of leadership if understood and applied with a sense of purpose and strategy. There are countless books and articles on how to succeed in business and life, but so far as I know, none of them look at this unseen power that companies, individuals, even nations, have at their disposal. But any really successful team, any powerful individual, consciously—or unconsciously— employs the power of invisibility as part of a successful strategy. If one pauses for a moment to think of certain powerful companies in our midst, my point may become clearer. Consider a company like Xerox, for example.

Xerox began years ago working with a big, clunky copying machine that had more parts than a medieval drawbridge. Other companies in the field were producing copying machines as well. But Xerox took a new copying process called xerography and give it a corporate name. It then developed a brilliant marketing strategy based on that name. All the while, it kept refining its machine so that it became less unwieldy, cheaper, more accessible to the general public. Meanwhile, other companies were moving along with their copying machines as well. But Xerox had an advantage: I call it the power of invisibility. Its name, its successful marketing strategy, made it a household word in America, and before too long whenever someone wanted to get something photocopied, they naturally told themselves they were getting it "Xeroxed," even though the machine that copied their documents might have been produced by another company.

What Xerox accomplished through the power of invisibility was to swamp the field, to infiltrate the minds of customers and competitors alike, giving the company a huge advantage that went way beyond the actual resources and technology they had at their disposal.

Another example of invisibility working as a power in our lives that may be even easier to understand is in politics. For years, the United States was caught up in the Cold War with the Soviet Union. Why did the war remain cold until the Soviet Union collapsed? Was it because the United States was so superior militarily that it was assured of victory in any possible combat with the Soviets, or was it because the Soviet Union reacted to the invisible threat of devastating military power that confronted them every day? We may be thankful to invisibility for preserving the peace on both sides, because surely the sense we had of the Soviet nuclear arsenal—never used—was a restraint, a power, that kept our power in check. Likewise, rival nations across the globe have refrained from wars not because they love each other or because they have principled convictions about peace, but becasue the power of invisibility— the unknown, invisible consequences that would flow from aggression—keeps them in check. There are so many similar stories in business, sports, and everyday life that we may begin to formulate a few basic Russell Rules on the subject:

RUSSELL RULES

Rule One: Invisibility is an extra dimension, an "X factor" that can be used, if understood, in relationships on all levels, personal, corporate, collective. It allows the "invisible" person or company the chance to augment its power, to appear unexpectedly, to have the knowledge no one anticipated, to intimidate rather than to muscle the competition.

Rule Two: Invisibility can be used as a practical tool, but only at the point when we recognize that others may not see us as we are (or may not see us at all). When that is understood, when we make the conscious effort to see that we are not seen, we can then put ourselves into position to define ourselves on our terms. The ability to do this is fundamental in any successful relationship whether it is in business or at home.

Rule Three: Invisibility opens doors, creates opportunity where none seemed to exist before. When we are unseen, we have an enormous advantage in moving in, in doing things we wish or need to do, and in the process to change the very dynamic of existing, seemingly closed, patterns. When economic conditions, for example, suggest that it would be unprofitable to open a business in certain depressed areas of the country, a shrewd investor will see that the area being looked at was never seen, that tremendous opportunity may exist there. Think of Wal-Mart or the Fairway supermarket chain, which opened a very profitable store in Harlem, New York.

In my home, my parents were the rulers, no doubt about it. I did what they wanted me to do. They led, I followed. My mother protected me in this life. She was my shield and my guardian, she made the dangerous world I grew up in appear to be safe. She insisted that I keep distant from those who would harm me physically or verbally; she kindled my imagination, insisted the library was the place for me, as well as the church on Sundays (from eight in the morning till ten at night!). My mother taught me to stand up for myself, to use my brainpower on my own behalf. She followed me around from day to day even though she wasn't there. Wherever I went, she accompanied me even though she was somewhere else.

One day, when I was twelve, she became ill and was taken to the hospital. A week later she died, a complete and overwhelming shock. But even then, more strongly than ever, she stayed with me—in my thoughts, my goals, my aspirations. She appeared to me in dreams. Sometimes she was just an image; other times she talked to me as though she were there in the room with me, counseling me, advising me. Listen to your father, she would say, be aware of how hard he works, how much he cares; try to do the best at whatever you do, respect all people, even ones you don't like, acknowledge the common humanity you share with everyone. She could never have done this unless she had consciously set out to influence me in a specific way in her life. Whether she knew it or not, she intended to make sure her presence, her teachings, remained with me when she was not around. Nothing would have worked if I had perceived her as simply an authority, a lawgiver. She got into my life and stayed there because she had the power to make herself invisible so that I might all the while focus on my own life, on what I had to do to become responsible for my success.

I have often wondered what it was that gave her the power of invisibility, and the only meaningful conclusion I have come to is that it was love. The power of her love for me was that strong. And in some way, it was not exceptional in that devoted parents always seem to have this invisible power that follows after their children, helping them do for themselves what they most need to do to be happy and successful.

My father, in a very different way, has been a similar, positive influence. I was never quite as close to him growing up as I was to my mother, yet he followed me around, too, present when I was unable to see him. And I think he knew that very well.

I was always aware that my father loved me, but he never treated me like a "favorite," as my mother had. He was a disciplinarian. When we lived in Louisiana and I got out of line, my mother would strip the leaves off a good, flexible willow branch and whip me, and I pretended it didn't hurt so she would say "Okay. Wait until your father gets home." So my father was there even while he was still away at work. I used to watch the roads on those afternoons when I knew I had a whipping coming, waiting to see him come around the corner, but he was already there, he had been there for hours making me think harder and harder about the punishment I had coming. But my father's love for me was stronger than his arm, and that was an unseen presence in my life as well.

About five years ago, I had a most meaningful discussion with him. He was approaching eighty and still tough as nails. We talked about the way our lives had impacted each other. I learned from him then, for the first time, that he had attended every one of my high school JV and varsity games, even when I was the last man on the bench and didn't get a minutes's worth of playing time. He told me he had sat up in the back behind our bench where I'd be sure not to see him. I asked him why he did that and he told me he wanted to be there to lend me support without doing anything to put extra pressure on me. He wanted to be aware of what I was doing and going through, but he did not feel the need to physically make himself known. There is a lesson here for every manager. You need to know what is going on with your employees, but you do not always need to force yourself on them or even influence them. You have to trust them to operate on their own (that's why you hired them in the first place). The funny thing about this talk with my father was that this story of his didn't really surprise me. I always knew he had been my biggest fan. My father's encouragement was like a constant current of energy in my body.

I then reminded my father of something that had happened when I was in college. At that point, I was having success and he was regularly attending my games. It was in my junior year and we were 15-1 at the time. The team was at a reception of some kind that my father attended. A reporter walked up and asked how many losses I thought the team would have that year. Before I could get a word out of my mouth, my father interrupted, his voice full of passion, "They've already lost all they're going to lose." I heard his words and the feeling behind them. In a way, I was caught off guard. I wasn't at all surprised by his love and pride, but he was showing this visibly. I had gotten so used to my father's invisible presence of support that I was thrown off by seeing it and hearing it.

There's an old saying that love between parent and child always goes toward separation. Yes, that is true—with all the variations of pain and loss that may be involved—but this act of separation can be creative and loving. Children, if they are to become successful adults, must claim responsibility for their lives. For that to happen, parents must step back, become invisible enough for children to go their own way fully convinced of their independence.

> *Today I think of my father as the most successful person I know. My father's success is all about respecting himself and others to the point where he can step back, out of the way, and be present at the same time. Wherever I went, whatever I did, I knew he had conferred great power on me—just as my mother had—a power that very much shaped my life, my sense of responsibility.*

During college, I began to be much more conscious of invisibility as a practical concept, something that could be employed in a daily working situation. My workplace then was the basketball court. For example, K.C. and I, in tandem, and after considerable experimentation, devised a defensive ploy to deal with breakaways where the two of us would trail after the guy driving the floor for a layup. We had no chance to catch the player, but if we slapped the soles of our sneakers on the floor to make it sound as if we were right behind him, the player would somehow alter his drive to the basket. He might turn his head to see where we were, or he might veer one way or the other, giving us time to catch him. The guy was reacting to invisible defenders. We were not there, but we were in his head.

When I got to the Celtics and a real team was in place with top athletes at every position, with a coach and an organization dedicated to winning championships against first-rate competition, this technique grew into something that was more like a strategy. My awareness of the possibilities of invisibility grew.

In my first season, the Celtics really had six, not five, starters. Frank Ramsey, coming off the bench, was really a swing man, someone too tall to play guard, too short to play forward. But he was a great player, and making him sit might have been a really unsettling factor on the team. But what I saw was how the team made a virtue of it. Everyone knew that Frank, who could no more resist a shot than a moth could resist a flame, would get the ball up as soon as he got his hands on it. Other players, instead of resenting this, tried to help him out— because he was so good. If he came into a game and was hot, our chances for winning multiplied. Because of the way he was used, Frank was never a substitute but a mystical extra, out there with us all the time.

I saw what that did to other teams. They reacted as though the Celtics had six men on the floor against their five. Even while Frank was on the bench, opposing coaches and players began gauging their matchups, their substitutions, with Frank in mind. Imagine how insidious and unsettling that was! We gained tremendous advantage from this.

I began thinking constantly about the different ways invisibility might be expanded and put to use. I was the kind of player who loved figuring things out, using my knowledge to satisfy my physical gifts. I was never content to simply run and jump, shoot or pass. I wanted to use my gifts in ways no one had ever used them. I had goals, goals that had nothing to do with stats but that were targeted to single games and to a career. My main goal was to always play a perfect game every time I played. To do that, I told myself before each game that this might be the only chance I'd have, so I'd better make good use of it. When I missed perfection—as I always did—there was always the hope of it in the next game.

> *My best nights were rarely ones that showed up in the box scores. I was once asked to name the best game I ever played. I thought about a play-off game where I had something like thirty points and forty rebounds against the Lakers, but then I thought there were so many games where I had fewer rebounds, assists, and blocked shots, where I wound up scoring only eight or ten points, but where I was really far more effective. Those games were always ones where I knew I was in the heads of the players on the other side. I could see how they altered shots or refused to take them for fear that I was somewhere nearby—even though I wasn't. Sometimes during these games I'd be on the bench and watch this happen. It was amazing. Opposing players seemed to be looking for me even though I wasn't on the court.*

As a player, I believed in intimidation. I didn't want to just win games, I wanted to rob the other team of any sense of belief they had in their ability. I didn't want players thinking they could come back against us when they were down. Toward the end of my career, when I couldn't go forty-eight minutes, I had to guard Elvin Hayes, who at that point was young, strong, and tearing up the NBA. He was a great scorer and a really smart player. The first time I went up against him, my game plan was to deny him the ball. If he didn't get his hands on the ball, how could he score? I played him tight, fronted him, did everything I could to make it harder to get a pass into him. It was well into the second quarter and Hayes had taken only two shots. We were standing on the court lining up after a time-out and I casually said to him, "Hey, I heard you were supposed to be the main man, how come these guys don't pass you the ball?"

Those words somehow got to him. He gave me a little shrug, and then I noticed that he began to let up, to stop looking for his teammates to get him the ball. I didn't have to continue smothering him or do much of anything. He was taken out of his game for the rest of the way. When I wasn't close to him, he seemed out of it; when I went to the bench and he remained in the game, nothing changed. It was as if I were there draped all over him. I wound up being more in his head than on his back.

Even when I was most physically intimidating, I used the power of invisibility to help me. When I went to block a shot, for instance, I wanted to do it in such a way that I could surprise the other player. I would trail a guy who was going to the basket knowing that I would be able to go up with him and knock the ball away. But instead of going with him step for step, I would often take a long stride to the left so that when the player went up for his shot, I would be coming at him from an angle he wasn't anticipating. I wasn't supposed to be there. My jump, instead of coming from behind him, would be coming right at him from the side. I would not only be able to block his shot but do it in such a way that the ball would bounce off the glass or directly to one of our players starting up the other way. It was scary for other players to experience that, and they wound up constantly trying to adjust what they did on the court to keep clear of me.

Our opponents were not just intimidated by us. They were intimidated by the Boston Garden. At the heart of this book is the belief that there was no "mystique" to our eleven championships. We won them using the eleven lessons outlined here. But there was a mystique about the Boston Garden, a powerful invisible force that did some strange things to our opponents. Nothing epitomized this more than the floor we played on. The famous "parquet floor" was another one of those factors my teammates and I knew how to exploit. In reality, the floor was just a portable basketball floor. Over the years, however, it had slowly gained an almost mythical status among fans and opposing teams. It was a constant invisible presence.

The floor was made up of 247 panels and 988 bolts. The wood came from oak scraps collected from a forest in Tennessee. In reality, it was a contraption as much as a floor. Moving the ball from one end to the other was less dangerous than moving across a minefield but the floor presented plenty of dead spots that sometimes interrupted dribbling. There were gaps in the boards wide enough to stick a few quarters in side by side. Kevin McHale, the great Celtic forward from the 1980s, noted one time that "The parquet floor changes after every Bruins game. The dead spots aren't in the same places. There's no meter registering the amount of torque on each bolt. The Bull gang just screws 'em in." I don't know if opposing teams were intimidated by the mystique or the mistakes of the floor. It didn't really matter. The parquet floor was an invisible power that worked on the opposition, it gave them one more excuse to accept defeat.

Ironically, the skill level of play in the NBA made it easier to use invisibility as a weapon. One of the skills top athletes have that others don't have or even understand is their vision. Top athletes in any sport see differently from ordinary people. Talk to a great baseball player, someone like Willy Mays or Joe Morgan, and they will tell you strange things about the way they saw a baseball. Mays will talk about seeing a ball in slow motion when he made a great catch. Joe Morgan was once asked how he was able to handle a hundred-miles-per-hour Nolan Ryan fastball. Morgan said he never saw a hundred-miles-per-hour fastball; every fastball Ryan threw to him seemed to be coming in at seventy-five to eighty miles an hour. Joe said that he was able to "slow the ball down" so that he saw it differently.

This extra dimension of vision made me fully realize that I could actually take advantage of a great athlete's power to see by making myself invisible as surely as that guy who unwound the bandages from his head in that old movie. When I played against Oscar Robertson, for example, I thought for a while that he had 360-degree vision. He seemed to know where everyone on the court was at all times; he could thread a pass through the eye of a needle, through a football scrimmage of bodies. But he didn't really have 360-degree vision at all; he had this peculiar ability great athletes have to focus. Where an ordinary player would see whatever was in front of him and whatever his peripheral vision took in, a player like Oscar would be able to eliminate everything between him and the player he wanted to pass to or the area where he had to get to shoot or set up a play. His vision then narrowed like a laser beam. Within that beam he could slow down or speed up the action as need demanded. But then everything outside that beam wasn't visible to him! I realized his great seeing power made him blind! And that allowed me to work invisibly against him. I could move into these blind zones and attack the ball or the player without being seen.

Then, also, with very different goals in mind, I consciously tried to make myself invisible on my own team. Because my game was always to get the best out of my teammates, I wanted them to forget about my being on the floor and to concentrate on what they had to do. Sometimes, if I was really doing my job, it was as if I were not even out there. I remember once, during a time-out, Red turned to me and ordered me back into the game. I had been on the court all the while. A mediocre coach's first thought is that if he did not notice one of his players out there on the court, then surely that player was doing nothing to help the team. But Red was never one to accept conventional thinking. He knew the power of invisibility in my game, and he respected it a great deal. I never once heard from Red that my play wasn't contributing in some way to our success.

I knew how to use this power not only as a player but also as a coach. In my last year with the Celtics, in our final championship series against the Lakers, we were trailing by one point with eight seconds left in the fourth game. I called a time-out and gathered the players at the bench. We knew what we had to do, there were no plays to diagram. I had called time to take myself out of the game and to get our five best jump shooters onto the floor.

When the game resumed, the inbounds pass went to Sam

Jones, who was always our first option for a last-second shot. Sam moved toward the side, off a pick, to get off his shot. Only he slipped on a wet spot as he was about to release the ball. He told reporters later that what went through his mind as he was falling to the floor was that he needed to get extra spin on the ball as he released it because there would likely be a rebound. If he missed the shot, he said, he wanted to make sure Russell (who, believe me, was on the bench) would have a chance to tip it in! It turned out Sam didn't need me. But the ball, with that extra spin on it, curled round and round the rim before it finally dropped in, giving us a one-point victory.

How can invisibility become a creative force, a technique for success, in your life? Begin with your personal relationships. If you genuinely love some people, if you have a powerful effect on their lives for good or ill, become aware that you will follow them around wherever they go. So use that for the good, for positive rather than negative ends. In corporate life, the goal of establishing your company carries with it the opportunity to extend resources and power beyond the limits of a budget to the possibilities conferred by invisibility, the hidden effect of your brand. Working for your success means making sure you are doing everything you can to work for your team's success. And then, also, the power of your own performance can be an invisible support for your coworkers, your teammates and colleagues.

The Celtics, quite specifically, understood the power of invisibility. Playing for the team was always the plan. You had to be willing to give yourself up—to make yourself invisible—if you wanted success. For example, when Bob Cousy came out of college, he could pass a ball behind his back, over his shoulder, looking the other way. No one had seen this kind of wizardry before. But Red was all over Cousy because too often those passes would catch teammates by surprise and they wouldn't be able to handle them. A good pass, Red was forever preaching, had to be caught. So Cousy nearly always delivered the ball so that players could do something with it. He had to keep his wizardry hidden until the right moment, when, suddenly, the spectacular, the magical pass, was exactly the right one, just what the winning moment called for. The magician was always present. The opposition knew it, tried to defend against it even when there was no need. Cousy remained invisible to baffle his opponents, to allow him and his team to have success.

At my height, it wasn't always easy to be invisible. It was especially difficult to use invisibility against a player like Wilt Chamberlain. But I did. Using ghost power against Wilt was truly one of the more joyful, if arduous, things I did during my time with the Celtics. Side by side, Wilt and I were as inescapable as China and India on a map. How could anyone avoid seeing us, paying attention to everything we did. Yet I am convinced that what I did in those many games against him was dependent on no one—including Wilt—seeing what I was really up to.

I mentioned before the different approaches each of us had to winning, the different ways energy flowed through us, the different logical conclusions we had come to about what we had to do for our teams. Wilt knew he had to be in the spotlight. He acted upon his intelligence, his awareness, his acceptance of being a man who was always in the spotlight. He couldn't help himself—any more than I could. I loved it that Wilt won scoring titles and my team won championships. I particularly loved those games when he would rack up forty points and thirty rebounds while I would get half those and the Celtics would come away with the game.

My game plan whenever I played Wilt was to keep him in the dark as much as I could. That may seem far-fetched, but it was crucial to the success I had against him. Because I knew Wilt as well as I did, I was always seeking to take advantage of his good nature. I did whatever I could to make sure I would never get him angry or fired up. My battle plan with him was always to keep him feeling as comfortable as possible with his own game. If he ever felt pressured or shown up, he would take notice and try that much harder. I was determined to make sure that never happened.

I was able to block Wilt's shots when I wanted. I knew that he liked to use his right hand, for example, and because I was left-handed, I didn't have to reach across my body to get a hand on the ball when he shot. If I slipped slightly to the left and went up with him when he took a jump shot, I knew I could knock it away—but most often I didn't want to do that because that was precisely the kind of thing that would get him going. Instead, what I tried to do was to play him just a little closer, force him to lean ever so slightly away from the basket, just enough to change his angle so that the comfortable shot he took was really slightly out of his range. Sometimes he would move back without my being on him, just because, in his body, he sensed I was there. If the shot went in, so be it; if it didn't, Wilt would never think that I had anything to do with his missing. At game's end, everyone in the arena saw what he had accomplished; my teammates, my coach, and I all knew what I had accomplished.

Through all the years I played for the Celtics, invisibility remained an essential component of my game and of any success I achieved. From the first day I turned up at practice to the last game I played, I quite deliberately cultivated an air of mystery among my teammates. I liked my teammates a great deal, more than I could ever show them then because I believed, as a matter of choice, that, in remaining unseen, who I was and what I did should never be confused. If ever I was taken for granted, as a player or as a person, my effectiveness as a teammate would have been compromised. I knew as deeply as I could that, when others could not see me—including people I cared about very much—I was stronger for it, stronger for myself and stronger for them.

Time for a game-ending sleight of hand on invisibility. Russell's Rules on the subject are visible and clear:

RUSSELL RULES

Rule One: Invisibility confers power. It is the "sixth man" on your team, the unseen but very present player who can consciously be employed in a winning strategy—in a company, in all relationships.

Rule Two: Use invisibility to shape how others see you. Create perceptions, don't just rely on them. The Boston Celtics, the Xerox Corporation, IBM, all have carried logos that have infiltrated the minds of competitors and of the public at large. You can be twice as big and three times as powerful even when you're on the sidelines, watching the action.

Rule Three: Invisibility opens doors when they are locked, it always creates opportunity for those willing to see.

Finally, unwind the bandages around your head, take a look around you, see everything, enjoy the untapped power that you have always had at your disposal. Watch what it can do for you and for your team. Think of invisibility as a plant: whatever beauty or ugliness it produces above ground for all to see, the roots that give it life are deep beneath the ground, far out of view, invisible, alive, drawing sustenance from the heart of the earth.

LESSON SIX

CRAFTSMANSHIP

CRAFTSMANSHIP IS ANOTHER WORD FOR QUALITY. IT IS also about getting the best results from your work effort. When we are creating a team we have to apply the same quality as a fine Swiss watchmaker. Craftsmanship comes out of intelligent hard work.

I hated practice. I never minimized, however, the importance of repetition in getting ready for a season. Your craftsmanship comes out of your dedication to your practice.

> *Success is a result of consistent practice of winning skills and actions. There is nothing miraculous about the process. There is no luck involved. Amateurs hope, professionals work.*

The three Russell Rules for Craftsmanship are as important to winning as any of the other rules in this book. Let me introduce them to you:

RUSSELL RULES

Rule One: Learning is a daily experience and a lifetime mission. I truly believe in the saying "We work to become, not to acquire." The more I learned, the more I knew I had to learn. In fact, as part of your daily experience I think it is critical to understand why you are succeeding and build on it. For example, I never watched film of what I did wrong. I always watched films of games where I played well so I could learn more about what I did to help the team win that game. In college, K.C. Jones and I worked on not only being the best in the country, we worked on being as astute as we could possibly be. The basketball court became our classroom, workroom, and laboratory. Whether it was learning how to force a certain shot that would result in a certain rebound angle, or how certain players would likely act in game situations, we wanted to understand the game at a level other players before—and I am not sure since—never approached.

Rule Two: Craftsmanship and quality are never an accident. Craftsmanship is the result of sincere effort, principled intentions, intelligent direction, and skillful execution. It could be said that craftsmanship represents the highest choice of many alternatives.

Rule Three: Make craftsmanship contagious. Players on great teams learn from each other. The lifetime of experiences we bring to each relationship is a gift to be shared. An entire team working to be the best will be the best.

What, precisely, is it in craftsmanship that is so valuable as a leadership skill? Why should doing something well necessarily put you one step ahead of your competitors or allow you to feel that your life is somehow better for it? In my own experience, the answer to those questions goes back to my father.

My father once told me that anyone who worked for three dollars an hour owed it to himself to put in four dollars' worth of work so at the end of the day he could look any man in the eye and tell him where to go. My father believed that you could feel a sense of security for giving more than what someone was expecting from you. I took my lead from him.

When I received my basketball scholarship to the Universiy of San Francisco, I directly attributed my getting that scholarship to following my father's advice and the understanding I had gained from him about craftsmanship. I rediscovered my father's words about the meaning of work, and I committed myself to learning everything I could to improve my game, to making myself the best basketball player on the planet. At that time, I wasn't much of a shooter, so, with the encouragement of my freshman coach, I spent hours in the gym shooting. Night after night, sometimes until midnight or one o'clock in the morning, I would take up to five hundred shots left-handed and five hundred shots right-handed, mainly hook shots, the kinds of shots a center would take. I'd swoop left and right, touching the ball off the glass or going straight for the basket. It was hard work, but I couldn't get enough of it. As I wrote in "Lesson Four," whether you love practice or not, you need to learn something new every time you go out there or else you won't get positive results. I loved what I was learning, and the payoff was acquiring skills I didn't have before.

When I began practicing these skills, I did not feel particularly comfortable going to my right because I was left-handed. But I kept shooting right-handed over and over again until, slowly, I began to have a feel for it. It was like taking piano lessons, when you reach the point where your right hand has to do something different from your left. If you have no real interest in lessons, you might give up at that point or continue in such a way that the skills you acquire will be adequate and no more. But if you love what you're doing, the very difficulty of what you need to do will drive you further, and the sense of accomplishment you gain will mean that much more. Weeks, months, tens of thousands of shots later, I became able to use both hands easily.

Because I was a center, I needed to understand how best to move my feet. The small moves a center makes in the post are all about footwork: where your feet are planted, when and how to shift them, how to take small steps rather than big ones, when to turn, what angle your body should take to the basket and to your defender. I wanted to be able to move in such a way that defenders wouldn't be able to outguess me, to either overplay me to my natural hand or drop back because they minimized my ability to score. I also wanted to be a threat whether I shot the ball or not. If I wasn't going to shoot, I wanted to make sure my movements would be more likely to confuse or tie up the guy guarding me, so that I might have better passing options or be in a better position to set a screen or to draw double coverage. I taught myself to have "smart feet" by running and moving, whenever I could, like a guard rather than a big man. Smart feet are the result of both brains and endless work.

Craftsmanship is inevitably linked to success, but, even

more, it is tied to leadership. The better you are at what you do, the more you set an example without words or memos for others to see and follow. Craftsmanship is *infectious* because it raises the standard. It is a funny notion, but many times if you refuse to accept anything but the very best, you often get it. In my opinion, craftsmanship needs to become an important part of your business culture. My father used to say, "If you don't do it excellently, don't do it at all." Besides your employees, craftsmanship becomes an important element of your institutional and product brands. I have often believed that anyone can cut prices, but it takes brains and commitment to make a better product. From the perspective of quality, there is as much craftsmanship in a Honda as there is in a Lexus, and because of that craftsmanship both cars are enormously successful.

I was a high jumper in college. I did it just for fun, and I had considerable success at it, but jumping became an integral part of my craft as a basketball player. Because I left my feet so often in defending, much against prevailing opinion and the specific instructions of my coach, I had to teach myself how to do this correctly and effectively. No one could teach me these things because no one was doing it this way. I knew that jumping could be a tremendous asset to me because I had that kind of power in my legs. The technical problem for me was what to do if I went for a fake. If I was up in the air and a player got past me, what, if anything, would enable me to recover?

I figured out that the way I landed determined what I would be able to do. If I landed straight-legged, I was lost. And most guys when they went into the air didn't think about the way they came down, they just let their feet guide them back to earth and there they were. But I discovered that if I came down with my legs in a flexed position, nine times out of ten I'd catch the guy who'd gone past me and I'd be waiting for him when he shot again, so he'd wind up saying to himself, "Where did he come from?" I worked on this. I kept practicing jumping and landing in a flexed position. I needed added power and agility for this as well. I devised an exercise for myself where I bounced up and down on my toes because that increased strength in my feet, ankles, and lower legs. I'd do this "bouncing" before practice, jumping and touching the rim thirty-five times.

I kept watching other players all the time, always trying to match their moves against what I could see myself doing. I noticed that when players went up into the air to take jump shots, for example, they didn't go as high as they could. Most players set up their jump shots so as to control the shots they could get, which meant that I had a tremendous advantage as a defender because I could go higher, as high as I needed, on my jump. A good shot always comes from the toes and then flows up through the body to the fingertips. And I observed then that for good shooters to get off good shots, they had to be in position to use their feet, their toes. They had to essentially square up to the basket, and if they didn't, if they were forced to turn to the side, for example, they would be less effective. So I taught myself to always move against a shooter in such a way that he would not be able to square up. If I was correctly positioned, I would be able to spring out or to the side so quickly a shooter would wind up altering what he did, taking a more difficult shot even when I had little or no chance of blocking it. In my time, they didn't keep statsitics for blocked shots (that started in 1973–74). But a few years ago, I was talking to Jack Ramsey, the veteran NBA coach who had seen many of my games, and he said he thought that I averaged double-digit blocked shots per game, and that for each of those blocked shots I forced shooters to alter what they were doing five or six times.

In high school and college, I read all the articles I could on basketball. I had stacks and stacks of magazines. I studied what players said, learned about their habits and idiosyncracies, and I remembered all of them. I pored over photographs of players, particularly ones whom I thought I might be playing against at some time, or players whom I simply admired, who I believed had something in their game I might be able to use.

> **When I got to the Celtics, I was a different kind of player. I was a center but I had the skills of a guard. I had through all those hours of work made myself into someone who could move in a new way from an old position. I felt my craft as a basketball player was growing. The next stage for me was to bring my craft from my individual success to my team.**

I knew that Red and my teammates might not immediately see everything in my game. If I were a golfer, my game would have been complete. But I was player in a team sport, and now I had a real team to play with. My experience would be the same as that of someone who was a top salesman and was then promoted to management. I had to shift my focus from becoming the best I could be to making my team the best it could be. I had no idea how much more I still had to learn.

I wanted to match my skills to the skills I saw around me. How to do that? How to take advantage of each player on the floor, how to make sure what I was doing would bring out the best in everyone around me? I saw right away how impressive the Celtics' fast break was and how brilliant Bob Cousy was in leading it. My first job, therefore, was figuring out what I could do to trigger the break. That meant devising a way to get Cousy the ball off the backboard as quickly as possible. Sounds easy, but it wasn't. If your big man goes up, gets the ball, comes down with it, plants, moves his arms from side to side to make sure no one is going to steal the ball, there will be no fast break. Or if the center is a little quicker, comes down, turns, looks, throws an outlet pass, that extra second or two consumed will still allow defenders time to get back.

Because I had worked so hard on my jumping and because I had strong peripheral vision, I could see on either side of me when I went up for a ball. If Cousy was positioned in one area when I went up for the rebound, I could take the ball off the backboard and pass it to him in the same motion. All I needed from him was the color of a jersey in a familiar area of the floor so that when I made this single movement of jumping, twisting, and passing, I would not be throwing the ball away. Left side, white shirt (on the road, green shirt). I could do this so quickly defenders would often be standing flat-footed watching the play from the backcourt as we completed the break with an easy basket. I got more out of being able to execute that than I did out of awards and public recognition. It was a joy to perform that move perfectly and successfully time and time again.

The same was true when it came to running our plays. I prided myself on how much I could do. In the Celtics half-court game, all plays went through me. For them to work, every guy on the floor had to be in motion. Each of us had a part to play, each had to be ready to become a second, third, or fourth shooting option. Our plays required an ongoing, active basketball craftsmanship where the movement of one player would immediately be understood by every other player. My job was to see every move by every player, to coordinate and process it as if my brain were a computer, and then to make the right pass.

There are eleven different kinds of passes from the center position: high post pass facing the basket, low post pass with your back to the basket, bounce passes left and right, hook pass left, hook pass right, jump pass, pass behind your back, over-the-shoulder pass, step pass, which changes the passing lane, and lob passes over chasing defenders. I always had to keep in mind who the player was I was passing the ball to, who was defending him, where that defender was positioned. I had to know how different players saw the ball when I made a pass. My teammate Satch Sanders, for example, wore glasses. He was a wonderful player, highly intelligent, and could move well without the ball, so he usually found ways to get himself open. But, when he wore contact lenses, he couldn't see below his waist. So any pass that came to him at his knees or even at thigh level, he would not be able to handle well.

The joy I got was that my passes almost always were the right ones, never spectacular, always delivered so that the player on the receiving end would be in a position to do something with it. If I got the ball to a shooter who had only a second of daylight, I made sure I sent a "dead" ball, a pass with a lot of backspin so that as soon as the player caught it, he would be able to get off a shot. I loved making passes in from out of bounds because I could see each of my teammates so distinctly in the rush of bodies moving this way and that. By then, because I had acquired enough technique, I could slow those bodies down in my mind's eye before I released the ball.

Playing defense with a real team was an even greater challenge, but had an even more satisfying payoff in terms of seeing how much other teams became intimidated or were thrown off their game. When I came to the Celtics, I believed that it was possible to win games with defense alone. My team made me a prophet in my own time.

It's much harder to play defense because you're not handling the ball, and a team has to be even more precisely coordinated in what they do. On offense, it's possible to take a break, to stand around a bit, let other players take over. On defense, if you take a break, a good offensive team will burn you. On the other hand, when you and your teammates are all doing the job—and you're all that good—the great reward is watching the other team slowly suffocate.

A really good defensive team uses its intelligence to an extraordinary degree as well as its agility and muscle. Every move you make on defense has a consequence for your teammates. For example, if you see that the player you're guarding wants to go left to shoot, inevitably a defender will try to do something to force him to go the other way. But in doing that, the offense will take note and do something else, and it's up to the defenders to pick up on that. Everyone on defense has to move and make exactly the right counteradjustments for the team game to work. If double-teaming leaves someone open, for example, it is important for the double-team to come together in such a way that the guy with the ball won't be able to see the open man. We perfected that on the Celtics.

Each team, each player, is different. On team defense, it is absolutely necessary to know your opponents as well as your teammates. The way they move, they way they pass the ball, the way they move without the ball, are all part of what must be taken into account for the defense to work. On my team, because we were so conscious of team defense, we were especially mindful when we saw good defense thrown at us. The challenge to break it down was great, but the rewards when we were able to do it were oh so sweet.

The Knicks in the late 1960s, for example, had one of the best defensive units in the game. In 1969, we faced them in the play-offs after they had taken us six times in seven regular-season games. Before our series against them in the Eastern Divisional Finals started, I took home the statistics from the regular season and studied them. I was aware that the Knicks had done a great job of closing us down, and I wanted to see if anything in the numbers would give me a clue. As a player and a coach, I didn't look at statistics the way sportswriters and fans did. I wasn't interested in who scored most, got the most rebounds or assists. I was after clues that would let me see patterns, what it was that enabled the Knicks to succeed against us. The stats, this time, revealed something startling about the Knicks' defense.

I noticed that in each of the regular-season games against them, I had taken no more than five or six shots. Now the guy guarding me and the backbone of the Knicks defense was Willis Reed. Because I hadn't been shooting much, Reed had been free to help out on defense. He had been able to leave me safe in the assumption that I wasn't likely to get the ball and shoot.

The Knicks gained from this in the way they used Walt

Frazier in tandem with Reed. Frazier, a great player who really never received enough credit, was as good a defensive player as there was. So Frazier, when Willis moved away from me to help out, would go after a likely shooter and drive him toward Reed. Again and again, our best or most likely shooters found themselves stifled or hemmed in. How to defeat that? The answer for the play-offs was clear. Don't give Willis Reed that kind of freedom. To break the defense, I needed to shoot the ball. It was as simple as that.

So in the first game of our series, instead of taking five or six shots, I took twenty-three. And we beat the Knicks—in New York—108-100. Reed found himself pinned to me, unable to drift away to help out. Frazier and the rest of the Knick defenders were then unable to keep up with our shooters. The Knicks ran the same defense against us that had been so successful during the regular season, but we had found a way to break it.

Teams that play at the skill levels of the NBA constantly adjust and readjust, and the same was true in this series. The Knicks, just because they were so good defensively, soon saw what we were up to and adjusted by rotating defenders to help out Reed so that my scoring would be limited. But as soon as the Knicks did that, we adjusted, too. I now had open men I could get the ball to. In the sixth and final game, the Knicks had adjusted again and we went back to the old pattern, but by then it was too late. The game was over and we won.

Team craftsmanship is akin to going from the stage where you are working by yourself on an invention, building a car or a plane, then having to apply what you've learned to the assembly line and to strategies of the marketplace where your craftsmanship has a direct payoff in terms of winning. Craftsmanship can never work by numbers alone, by connecting X's and O's on a chalkboard or by looking at videotape.

As a coach, Red Auerbach would seem to an uneducated observer hopelessly out-of-date today. He didn't watch film or video. He didn't scout other teams. He didn't go around measuring body fat with calipers and getting digitalized readings of a player's reaction times and muscle strength. There were no team meetings to inform us what had happened in our opponent's last three games. What Red relied on was his players' skill and passion. He counted on our active ability to think things through and then come up with whatever we needed to do to win. Winning was our assembly line, championships were our automobile. I have no particular attachment to the "good old days," to the automatic assumption that some old-timers make that everything back then was great and everything going on today is lousy. I just believe that Red understood craft. He understood perfectly how the success of a winning team depended on individual skills and team work.

Red was a mathematician as well as a basketball man, and he drew on that as a coach. Mathematics allowed him to solve problems, to ask the right questions—even ones that couldn't be answered. It enabled him to see differently. He was forever watching geometric patterns on the floor, picking up the way the flow of the game changed. He was constantly playing with numbers. He was obsessed with what he could do to change the odds of a game in our favor. For example, he'd try to do things early in a game to get us five easy baskets. If we had gotten the five easy baskets, he'd say we had automatically changed the odds because the other team then needed at least five hard baskets to beat us. Five was a number in Red's mind: five baskets, five outstanding plays, five free throws, five anything that would tilt the game in our favor. Red made substitutions according to numbers, too. He wanted patterns of players on the floor at all times, a balance of shooters, rebounders, defenders. If the pattern was broken, the balance was lost, the team was vulnerable. Even in the final minutes of games, the abacus in Red's mind was clicking away: "Okay, we've got three minutes left, we're up by ten, that means if we play good defense and don't throw the ball away, we need three more baskets." Or he'd bark, "They have to score three out of the four times they have the ball, we need to score only one in four." A manager in a fast-moving, highly competitive industry like the retail food industry, for example, faces similar challenges. To stay a step ahead, the manager of a supermarket chain has to juggle inventory, sales prices, warehouse supplies, personnel, down to the wire if he expects to stay that one step ahead. Certain goods that are not available from wholesalers will not become sale items, but others will. Knowing exactly how many items will beat a competitor's price that week, knowing just how much to order so that perishable goods are never backed up, all of these choices carry the pressure of the game's final minutes but also, provided the manager really understands the significance of patterns and odds, a tremendous likelihood of winning.

But Red left all of the doing to us. He treated each of us as the individuals we were. Some players he rarely talked to, while other players he took aside and coached. When he left a player alone—such as K.C. Jones or Cousy or me—it was because he knew that the player was doing exactly what he needed to do for himself and the team. When he coached a player— such as Sam Jones—it was never with the sense that he was going to show him skills the player didn't possess but only to support him in using them.

> *For a player to experience the game on a level where he has to use all of himself, where he is, in effect, a problem solver as well as a body, constantly committing himself all out to the possibilities of the moment, creating chances and opportunities for himself and his team, is to experience the game at the highest level of creativity. Craftsmanship at this level is about artistry.*

The idea that there is one way, a correct way, a one-size-fits-all way to do things is as mistaken as the eye of a video camera that sees everything but not the significance of it. Craftsmanship is a lot like finding your leadership style. There is no one way to get there. Each player has to find within himself what craft is really about, what it is in craftsmanship that is individual and distinguishing. A team player applies all that, and in the applying creates success for his team.

A word more about the game I have known so well. One time in Los Angeles during the lockout, I was talking with Shaquille O'Neal, someone I have great respect for as a player and as a person. We got into a conversation about foul shooting. His critics never let him forget how much he hurts his team by not making free throws. I told him by all means to keep working on the craft of foul shooting, but to always keep the focus on what he was doing overall to help his team win games. If he got sidetracked worrying about shooting fouls, it would only undermine what he did best. Shaq is a player who offers far more to his team than his ability, or lack of ability, to convert free throws. He has a complete game to offer. He is a mammoth presence in the middle of the paint. No one can stop him from scoring. If his opposition fouls him again and again, he has the strength to break that strategy eventually. He is a much better passer than people give him credit for. His game is full of possibilities, and all he really needs to remember is to use all of himself and not let himself get sidetracked. The Lakers won a championship in 2000, the first with Shaq in the middle, not because of his foul shooting, but because he found a way to use all his skills to help his team become a winner.

Personally, I found a great thrill in using my craft as fully as I could. But it was always about winning. I loved those times when a situation looked absolutely hopeless and yet I could still do something to turn things around. I probably broke up thirty-five to forty three-on-one breaks in my career, for instance. The feeling of joy and accomplishment I felt after each one of those defensive gems was contagious. I wanted to do it again. I remember once that we were a single point down in a regular-season game against Philadelphia with twelve seconds left. Archie Clark of the Sixers had the ball in the frontcourt and was dribbling out the clock. I was the only player near him. I knew I had no chance to take the ball from him. He had so much room he could have just stood still with the ball. So I stared at him—and he stared back at me, smiling. What followed happened so quickly it deadens out in the writing. My mind flashed on this player; I told myself, "Archie Clark is a scorer who is more inclined to take a layup than a jump shot. If he had a shot, he would be more comfortable taking a layup . . . so what I'm going to do is turn my back and start to walk off the floor like I've given up." I did this—and he did exactly what I hoped he would do. He drove to the basket for an easy layup. But there I was, waiting for him! I blocked the ball, called time-out. There were three seconds left. We took the ball out in frontcourt. Havlicek passed in to me down low; I dunked. We won in regulation.

There's an old saw about doing your job and letting go of the results. It's grounded in deep truth. I was always more interested in the doing, in the craft of playing, than I ever was in rings on my fingers. At the height of my game, what I found was the joy of my life. I remember one time in a game when I felt I could do no wrong and everyone else on the court—on both teams—was playing equally as well as I was. This went on for five, maybe six uninterrupted minutes before the referee finally blew his whistle and called a foul on the other team. I was furious! My teammates looked at me as if I were nuts. But all I could think of was that this beautiful plateau of accomplishment, flight at another almost perfect level, had been interrupted. I had almost forgotten that that whistle meant a couple of extra points for the Boston Celtics.

Craftsmanship, of course, applies in all situations, whether people belong to a team or are working for themselves. Hal Dejulio, who recruited me to USF, was a great insurance salesman. I asked him "How do you sell so much insurance?" "I don't sell insurance," he answered, "I help people buy it."

> **Craftsmanship is a way in to what's best in yourself. The real mastery is always of yourself.**

Parents, for example, say they love their kids. But parents who really care are always looking for ways to make their children's lives better, to strengthen the family unit they all belong to. The art of parenting means that you reach beyond just saying to yourself that you love your kids. You need to find what it is in yourself that allows that to happen. How do you show your love for your children? How do you build your family into a model that works? When I was a single parent, having to raise a twelve-year-old girl, I had left my job with the Seattle Super-Sonics. My friends expected me to pack up and leave Mercer Island and the state of Washington. I had no intention of doing that. My daughter was in one of the best public schools in the country. She had a real and ongoing life of her own. There was no thought of moving. And it wasn't a sacrifice. I wasn't about to visit my troubles—that I was out of a job—on my daughter. My "craft" in parenting meant recognizing that and acting accordingly. My job was to establish a routine, everyday life between us that would allow her to feel safe and comfortable. You share your life with your children, you provide for them, you allow them to be who they are while, at the same time, offering them guidance and protection. It's the most delicate—and rewarding—of arts because it is about love. It goes back to that old saying that it's not what you give but what you share.

So, in summary, let's look back at a few pertinent Russell Rules for Craftsmanship:

RUSSELL RULES

Rule One: Learning should be a daily experience and a lifetime mission. Michelangelo said, "I have offended God and mankind because my work didn't reach the quality it should have." I always believed if Michelangelo felt that way, then I would always strive for the best because anything else would not be enough.

Rule Two: Craftsmanship and quality are never accidents. In lesson three, on listening, I talked about the importance of careful language selection to get folks to listen more effectively. Well, think about replacing the word *quality* with *craftsmanship* and reintroduce it as an integral part of your brand.

Rule Three: Make craftsmanship contagious. Craftsmanship and teamwork go hand in hand; one cannot happen without the other. If others see the care and dedication that you put into your job and into winning, they will follow. Accomplishing that is a true mark of a winning leader.

One final thought. Because I have gotten so much joy from the things I have done in my life, it has sometimes been hard to think that joy itself is a leadership quality. But it is. When a leader is obviously passionate and joyful in what he or she does, that is inevitably communicated. It sets a tone, a standard in which winning is not the only thing but the most natural thing in the world.

PERSONAL
INTEGRITY

"TRUST THE TELLER AND YOU'LL TRUST THE TALE." THIS quote, which I first heard from a close friend whose father used to always say it, is at the heart of this chapter on personal integrity. To me, that quote means that personal integrity is always, first and foremost, about trust and truth.

To reach any level of understanding of ourselves we must examine who we are and at least understand and accept the many aspects of our individuality. I do not usually pay much attention to names of companies, but I know this guy Rob Smith, the CEO of a Bluemont, Virginia, marketing company called Focal Point. I loved that name because of the imagery it evoked. A focal point is where light converges through a prism or lens and results in a multitude of colors that exit on the other side. I believe that we are a blend of colors, and that this blend of colors comes from a single light. I call that light personal integrity.

A friend of mine who is a minister once told me a story from the Bible that is a wonderful metaphor for understanding personal integrity. The story tells of a king who heard of the

Hebrew leader Moses that he was a kind, brave, and munificent chieftain. Curious about this man, the king consulted his astrologers and asked his spiritual advisors to study a portrait of Moses. They told the king that Moses was cruel, greedy, and self-centered. The king's curiosity was now stirred, so he went to see Moses for himself. He found him to be a good man, in fact, a very good man. The king then related what his advisers had told him. Moses listened intently and then told the king that he agreed with what the astrologers and phrenologists had told him. "They saw what I was made of, but they couldn't tell you how I struggled against that so that I would become what I am."

Integrity is assuredly not an easy thing to define because it is so individual at its core, yet it is perhaps the single most essential quality needed by a leader. Integrity is about the beliefs, attitudes, and behaviors that go into how we make decisions, how we conduct ourselves in our day-to-day lives, who we are in the workplace and at home. Because individuals really are just that, Russell's Rules here are about ways to help you establish your own standards of integrity:

RUSSELL RULES

Rule One: Take responsibility for everything you do. The first day of practice is the beginning of a championship season. The first memo in the morning is the beginning of the introduction of a new idea.

Rule Two: Stand behind the choices that you make. No leader can manage with "buts." That means committing yourself to understanding what goes into a choice: the information you have at your disposal, the competing arguments, everything that you will need to provide you with a willingness rather than an excuse to make a choice.

Rule Three: Be fully present in whatever you are doing. That means giving all of yourself to a task at hand. That sounds easy enough but it isn't, because there are so many ways to back off, to move away, to let others do for you what you know you have to do for yourself and your team.

The most essential and common behavior integrity demands of us is responsibility. In its essence, that means being able to own what it is you do. That implies that your actions and words will be filled with self-awareness. That you will take the pains to see consequences, possibilities, liabilities, opportunities, in whatever you do—and accepting them rather than feigning surprise or ignorance when what happens subsequently produces a result less desirable than what you wished for.

For me, the most succinct way I can talk about taking responsibility is to say that I always regarded the first day of practice as the beginning of a championship season. On my team, those who showed up in shape, ready to play and to give an all-out effort, understood this principle. They took their responsibilities seriously.

Decision-making is another crucial component of integrity. In business, life, or sports, we constantly need to make choices. When we bring all of ourselves to the task, when we see the different sides clearly, the competing interests, pressures, inducements, when we satisfy ourselves that we know what may flow from each aspect of a potential decision, then and only then will we be forcefully engaging our sense of integrity when we make what we believe will be a positive choice.

Finally, the test of integrity is how it stands up in day-to-day life, in the workplace, with colleagues, employees, bosses; at home with spouse and children; anywhere you find yourself with others where your conscience must be active for you to be fully present. It is crucial for you to understand the expectations, demands, pressures, of others, to coherently evaluate a new job, a new client, a new friend (or an old one), your own children: a daughter just becoming a teenager, say; a son who has just gotten a driver's license and can't wait to get out on the road. Integrity always comes back to this point in reality where you are called to be fully present.

A leader who lacks integrity will sooner or later be leading no one; a follower who is without it goes nowhere. Integrity is what allows us, wherever we find ourselves in life, to stand behind our words and actions. Integrity allows us to look in the mirror and be comfortable with the person looking back at us. Integrity is our guide through the swampland, our most trusted friend and most reliable critic both, our own personal Geiger counter.

The most obvious place integrity comes up or fails to is in the workplace. Shoddy goods, shortcuts, selling out, insider trading, stealing, cheating anyone—it's all there in the big

book of what we've done. Lack of integrity in the workplace is
so common the question to ask may well be is it possible to
avoid it, is it the system rather than the individual we're really
talking about? It's the sort of question that makes me think
about basketball in my day and the game today.

In my years the NBA consisted of eight teams. There are
twenty-nine today. There are a lot more players today than in
the 1960s. The rules and regulations make it possible for a
player to hang around in one town for a few years and then
move on, saying good-bye to his teammates and fans as though
they were all just commuters riding shoulder to shoulder for a
few crowded stops. Franchises spend record amounts of money
to woo away other teams' best players. Agents, who may not
even like the game but who have more economic leverage
than bankers and financial moguls, step in and negotiate the
future success or failure of whole franchises. What are we to
make of this? Is it possible for a player, coach, or owner to have
any integrity within such a system? My answer is, of course it is.

First, I want to answer a question that people keep asking
me, whether I would have preferred to play in this era when I
could, obviously, have earned so much more money. I know
that I could have commanded just about any price if I played
today. But I have never considered any other time better than
the time when I played. You cannot have a better tomorrow if
you are going to think about yesterday. I have nothing but the
most positive thoughts about today's game. Someone once said
to me that today's game was lacking because "they don't play
like you guys did." He was right. But neither did all the teams
that played before I got to the Celtics and neither did all the
teams that we used to beat.

In no way would I trade my years for what I might find

today, because to do so would mean turning my back not only on my own team and teammates, but most of all, on my own experience. I was profoundly happy playing with the Boston Celtics when I did. Happiness or personal satisfaction, to me, it almost goes without saying, is an ineveitable by-product of personal integrity.

There was one year when Wilt Chamberlain secured a contract for $100,000. A six-figure salary was a big deal at the time. No one in the league earned more money than him. Everyone was talking about it—and especially in Boston, where people were wondering what I would do. My answer was simple. It was simple because I enjoyed playing for the Boston Celtics and because I knew who I was. I loved being where I was and doing what I was doing. I submitted my contract demand to the Celtics: $100,001. One dollar more than Wilt. They agreed.

Money issues were as real on the Celtics as they were on any other sports team, but somehow they were handled differently. Frank Ramsey was our sixth man and because he was not a starter, according to prevailing budgeting practices in the league, he could not command as much in salary as any starting player. So, Frank bypassed Red, who was the team's general manager as well as coach. On the last day before the team broke at the end of the season, Frank stopped by Walter Brown's office. He asked Walter's secretary to provide him with a blank contract that he then signed and left behind, knowing that Walter's good-heartedness would take care of the rest. And he was right. Year after year, Frank never talked contract with anyone in the organization and always got enough to make him happy.

The important choices we make in our lives are never clear-cut. There are good reasons in many situations to go one way or another. Yet the ability to choose wisely or correctly is so fundamental to building success, to exhibiting true leadership, that it sometimes seems as if we are being asked to walk a high wire without a net below us.

The reason basketball players as well as athletes in other professional sports, as well as entertainers, writers, artists, etc., can get caught on the high wire really has little to do with money. It has to do with personal integrity and how it impacts decision-making. In today's market, decision-making is most often turned over to others, to agents, promoters, personal and financial advisers who have an expertise in law and finance that players do not have. The world of high finance is bewildering, confusing, even boring for someone who is really interested in just lacing up his sneakers and competing. The problem, of course, is that in turning over this bewildering mess to someone else, you are in effect turning over the power to act to someone else. That person may indeed make all the wise choices that could possibly be made on your behalf—but it won't be you making the decisions that most affect your life.

In my view, anyone who needs an agent or representative must thoroughly familiarize himself or herself with all that will be involved in making key decisions and ultimately take responsibility for every important decision. If it is left up to someone else to tell you what is best for you, you might as well listen to him or her because you will have no opinion yourself. If you are a CEO and you depend wholly on your chief financial officer to make decisions about budgets and investments, who then is really making the decisions that decide the future of the company? Now I'm not saying that the system of agents and advisers has to be scrapped in order for someone to hold on to his or her integrity. Big money is not ruining our sport, as so many believe, and I do believe that players should benefit as much as anyone. Integrity, however, forces people to take responsibility for themselves.

Integrity is so basic and so easy to misunderstand. It is all too easily mistaken for rigidity. Millions of people the world over live their lives by commandments and decrees. That has nothing to do with integrity. The Bible tells us Thou Shalt Not Kill, but all too many of those who swear by the Bible also believe in capital punishment. Our presidents are never more popular than when they send the troops off to war. People strictly and unthinkingly adhere to laws that tell them how to dress, eat, bathe, worship, behave—or else forgo the blessings of the divine or even the protection of the state. None of that has to do with integrity. Integrity always comes from within and, unlike dogma, always proceeds across a no-man's-land of doubt, fear, and contradiction where the only reliable guide is fidelity to oneself.

Many years ago, during the Vietnam War, Muhammad Ali decided to resist the draft as a conscientious objector. Because he was the heavyweight champion of the world and an outspoken, young black, his decision created a furor. Some accused him of being a traitor, a Communist, or worse. Some saw him as a great hero, a symbol of the antiwar movement itself. There was more pressure from without on that young man than if he had been in the way of an avalanche. What he thought and believed in the quiet of his own mind, his own integrity, was really the issue. With so much raining down on him, what did he really believe, what was he really willing to do for himself, what did he understand about what he might be giving up or gaining? He was facing five years in jail and the loss of everything he had built for himself in his career.

At that time, my friend Jim Brown organized a group of other well-known black athletes, including me, to go visit Ali. Our purpose was to lend him support—not necessarily for taking a stand against the war but for the right to make a key decision on his own behalf. We wanted him to know that whatever he decided, we would be behind him. We wanted him to know we were there as friends, not advisers. As much as possible, we urged him to forget the abuse and the praise coming down on him and to focus only on what he knew to be right or wrong. We wanted to convey to him a sense of trust and confidence in his beliefs and heart. He was out there on that high wire. It was not possible for anyone else to help him across it, only to encourage him to trust his own ability to do what he had to do.

We went to Cleveland to see him. I'm not sure to this day what I expected to see, perhaps a man out there by himself, overwhelmed and in peril of losing everything. Instead, the man I saw was utterly confident and at peace with himself. There was not the least hint in his makeup that he was wrestling with anything. I saw a man who was free. I was amazed by how confident he was, how much he was at ease with the decision he had made. His confidence had none of the show that he regularly put on before his fights but was such that you could not escape believing him. In spite of all the pressure and difficulty he was facing, he did not need us or anyone else to support him in the decision he had made. He had acted from his own integrity.

Of course, most of the decisions we make are not as dramatic. Much of what we are forced to decide for ourselves comes through layers of compromise. If we accept this position in the company, it will mean a bigger office, more pay, more time off, but it will also mean having to relocate to Utah or

New York. We may act with integrity in making necessary compromises. Same with the CEO who knows that his company's bottom line will improve with a string of cost-cutting measures such as plant closings, firings, eliminating divisions. He may act with integrity by making compromises so that he can save some jobs, keeping some people in place even though the bottom line may suffer.

In personal life, compromise occurs all the time and is a necessary aspect of life. Relationships demand it. We can't get what we want all the time without coming up against the conflicting demands and desires of others we care about. People we love, our spouses, our children, our dearest friends, have desires and needs of their own that can conflict with what we want. What do we do? The usual adjustment is compromise. And that is not bad. Intimate relationships especially most often involve a fundamental compromise with loneliness. We make those compromises so that we may find some balance between the desire to be as free as a nomad, hungry as a circling hawk, dependent as a wounded soul seeking solace and comfort.

In our own minds, the truth changes. What we know today may be different from what we tell ourselves tomorrow. Anyone who has lived as long as I have knows plenty of people who were waving one banner in their youth but who are today waving the banner of the opposition with as much passion. One of my favorite sayings is a remark attributed to Gandhi, a man who, to me, exemplified the full power of integrity. "I do not concern myself with being consistent," he was supposed to have said. "I only concern myself with being consistent with the truth as it reveals itself to me." The really interesting question to me is how we find the truth in ourselves. What can it be when it can shift or change appearance or become even its opposite over time? How are we to trust our own integrity in a world that does not stop for us, where change and compromise are inevitable, and where decision-making, especially in the face of extreme pressure, can make us think we are on a high wire where our lives are in peril?

My answer goes back to my youth, to my family, to the people whose lives even today are examples for me. My grandfather and my father both used to say that every person had a line inside them that no one could cross. And that it was up to each person to learn about that line in themselves. No one could show them what it was, no one could make them defend it, but it was necessary to know that one could not live at peace with oneself if that line was crossed. There was a family story that told me about this line.

My grandfather was a short man, about five feet six inches. He had hands as large as mine and was raised without much education, knowing and talking to people who had been slaves. My grandfather worked for himself all his life, hiring himself out as a farm laborer, ploughing people's fields and so forth. The most important thing to him, he always said, was education, making sure that young people who came after him would have wider opportunities than he had had.

Once, when he was a young man, he decided that he wanted to build a schoolhouse for young black children in the rural area of Louisiana where he lived. He went to a lumberyard to buy some wood to begin building. Somebody at the lumber store wanted the pile of wood my grandfather had just purchased. My grandfather wouldn't turn it over. A quarrel broke out. "We're gonna come and get you tonight, boy!" the customer threatened. When a car full of night riders pulled up to his house that night, my grandfather was sitting in a chair out front with a shotgun across his lap. "First man who steps across the line onto my property I'll shoot!" he shouted. When one of these guys then stepped past the boundary post of the front yard, my grandfather fired the shotgun—and the men took off. And somehow never bothered him again. The line they had crossed was that boundary line I had learned about. My grandfather was prepared to give up his life rather than let that line inside him be crossed.

I saw the line in another way in my father's life. When my mother died, my father, brother, and I took her body back to Louisiana from Oakland. While we were there for the funeral, my aunts got together to decide, as was the custom in black families when a matriarch died, which one of them would raise the children. One of the aunts said she would take me, another aunt said she would raise the other. But my father, despite prevailing custom and even knowing that my aunts were good women, wasn't about to give us up. My father told them it made no difference to him what they decided because he was taking us back to California and was going to raise us himself. A man can't raise kids by himself, raising kids was women's work, what was he thinking, what was he doing? They would have needed an earthmover to budge my father. They had come against that line in him that just could not be breached. He told my aunts he intended to raise his own son because that was the promise he made to my mother before she died, and he would spend his last breath sticking to his word.

That was not the end of it, either. My dad, at that point, had a fairly lucrative income from the truck business he had built up over the years in California. But his business often took him away from home, sometimes for days at a time. That created a dilemma. How would he be able to maintain his business and responsibly look after his own children? His answer surely roused a hornet's nest of contradictions in him, but his own sense of integrity guided him. He told himself that to responsibly raise his children he had to be there for them every day. At what he knew would result in a considerable financial loss, he then sold his business—the four trucks he had been able to acquire, the equipment, the shipping contracts, everything, and took a nine-to-five job in a local foundry. His hours allowed him to be home in the morning when his kids went off to school and to be back in time for dinner every day.

He made another choice at that time that also had to be most difficult. He decided to remain single until we were grown. I can only imagine what that was like for him. He was, by nature, a ladies' man. He was young, attractive, and full of energy. But he told himself that raising his children was his responsibility and no one else's. Rightly or wrongly, he told himself my mother could not be replaced—even though he would surely have welcomed the pleasures of companionship and domesticity for himself.

My father was not a martyr. He took real pleasure and pride in parenting. In the evenings we'd sit together and play card games (whist was our favorite), dominoes, and board games like Monopoly. We had lots of fun together, and my dad never made us think of what he was sacrificing for us. My father eventually did remarry—when my brother and I were grown and out of the house.

My father and grandfather were my teachers, and I soaked up their lessons simply by breathing, by being around them. No explanations were ever necessary. I knew at an early age that there was a line in myself that I would not allow anyone else to cross. I knew long before I was fully grown that I would be the one to decide what was important in my life and that I would need to pay strict attention to this inner place where the road went through that no-man's-land of uncertainty, contradiction, and compromise.

The everyday world we live in is the testing place for our integrity—our jobs, our marriages, our families, what we do with ourselves just trying to do the best we can. For example, when I graduated from high school, I did not know I had a basketball career in my future. I had never been the kind of player anyone really noticed. Scouts, if they saw me, didn't have much to say about me. Recruiters never visited my home. My goal was to go on to college, even though my family didn't have enough money. My plan was to get a job, save up enough, and eventually enroll in school. Reality dictated what I needed to do.

I got a job in the San Francisco naval shipyard. The objective of raising enough capital to go off to college seemed far off. It did not matter. What was right in front of me did. I had a job that required my attention and I learned a lot. Learning about the different kinds of metals that were used in shipbuilding became something I enjoyed. I needed to know—so I could do any job that came up—what metals were used in what aspect of construction, how the metals used in fabricating the hull, say, were different from those used in constructing the bridge, and so forth. The machinery used from day to day was new to me. I did everything I could to learn about the operation of these machines, to understand their functioning in the different tasks I had to fulfill.

At no time did I feel that my life was being shortchanged, because I was giving myself fully to what I was doing.

> *Many people ponder career choices when they are young and believe that unless they find exactly the right job or career path for themselves they will be eternally miserable. This is a fundamental mistake. What is essential is the inner commitment we make—the commitment of our integrity—to whatever it is we decide to do.*

We may decide to follow a path (as I did) that we will abandon for something else later on, but devoting ourselves to what we are doing at the time is invaluable to us because in that we are absorbing not only the potential of the moment but the power of our integrity being put to use. What I insist on is that integrity is a practical tool. It is surely our guiding light from within, but it is there to guide us, not to make us feel smug or superior. We have an extraordinary opportunity to make the most of any situation we find ourselves in if we are able to bring our integrity to bear on whatever we are called upon to do.

Ironically, I had a real test of my own integrity right at the point when basketball entered my life in a serious way. I had gotten a scholarship to the University of San Francisco for room, tuition, and board, with the promise that if I made the varsity in my sophomore season, I would get $30 per month in laundry money. At the end of my freshman year, when I had already been promoted to the varsity, one of the guys on the varsity let me know that he had seen the scholarship roster for the following year and that I wasn't going to receive any laundry money.

I asked my coach about this and he said, regretfully, that was so. I knew this had nothing to do with my coach, who was a decent man, but that line had been crossed as far as I was concerned. I went back to my dorm room, got down my suitcases, and began to pack. K.C. Jones came into my room and saw me packing. What was I doing? he wanted to know. I told him I was quitting school. Was I crazy? he wanted to know. No, I said, and explained to him what had happened. "You're leaving because they're not paying you thirty bucks?" "No," I said, "I'm leaving because they told me one thing and did another."

K.C., by then, knew me well enough to know that I meant what I said. He didn't hang around talking. Instead, he excused himself and went directly to the athletic office so he could tell our coach what was happening. Within minutes, both of them were back in my room. Why was I leaving? Phil Wolpert wanted to know. "Because I was lied to," I said. I told him the details. "The school made a choice to go back on what it promised me, so I'm making a choice to leave school."

My coach asked me to please wait for just a few minutes, and he hurried away. Before I finished packing, he returned and told me he had called the president of the university and explained to him what was happening. He told the president what I had said and added that if I followed through and quit, the school would be losing a very good basketball player. The president, he said, had insisted that there were just no funds available for the athletic department. But then the president said that there was one academic scholarship available, which would pay me $25 dollars a month, would I take that? That was light coming through the prism for me. I thought about it, didn't quite know what to do, but then, balancing everything out for myself, agreed to accept.

In the marketplace, integrity is a standard. The company that conveys a sense of integrity behind its product stands to gain enormous advantages. Take a company like Starbucks. The company began as a waterfront coffeehouse serving pastries and a really good cup of coffee. The owners of the company made that cup of coffee a standard. Everything they did went into making sure they had the best beans, the right machines, to produce quality coffee. When the company began to expand beyond the Seattle waterfront, there were, of course, many other decisions to be made. Licensing, distribution, determining when and where outlets should be opened. Should the growing company be confined to the Northwest? Should it expand to other areas? What kind of employment policies should be followed, who should be placed in key positions to make decisions that would affect bottom-line revenues? With all of that, the essential focus was on making sure the same good cup of dark-brewed coffee would be served at every single Starbucks outlet. The absorption was in a most fundamental aspect of the operation, in its most basic component—simple as that was. But this absorption in reality involved a fundamental act of integrity. It is all too easy to put aside the messy details of what we do in our lives, but attention to those details, surprisingly, comes from this place of integrity because what is really involved, consciously or otherwise, is an understanding of that line within oneself where what is on one side is okay and what is on the other is not.

In my life, I have found that integrity is its own reward. What you give you get back over and over again. I played with a team, for example, that exemplified integrity. Workplace, personal relationships, organization, everything from soup to nuts, made it easy for me to be true to myself and to gain from it. What I found with my team was that we all thought like winners. That meant that in each of us there was a standard, a line, that we upheld at all costs.

The Celtics were a great team and organization because this concept of inner commitment was understood at every level, in practical terms rather than theoretical ones. A stan-

> *Not long ago, I happened to thumb through some team pictures taken during my years in Boston. What I noticed was that I was the only player on the championship team of 1968–69, my final year, who also was on the championship team of 1956–57 (my first year). In all that time, through the eleven different championship seasons, the Celtics had made only one major trade. That meant the organization relied on its own skill in picking and developing players who would fit the system.*

dard was in place with the Celtics that team officials all understood. The standard was finding players who were athletically talented but who also came from successful programs, programs where it was far more likely for those individual players to produce in a winning system. What the Celtics, as an organization, wanted from their players was a standard of integrity.

In practical terms, this meant that in our system each player was in some way his own boss. That was built into what we did on the floor. Players had to think for themselves, to be aware that they had choices to make—where to move, how to set up, what they needed to do to take advantage in the moment and then to understand that whatever they did had a specific impact on teammates and opponents. Our few plays had so many variations because it was expected that the players would constantly use their creativity so that other teams could never successfully set up against us. We were a model of integrity because each of us so clearly understood who he was, what he had to do for himself and the team.

What is absolutely essential to understand is that integrity involves a willingness to be honest with oneself in any kind of self-assessment. Integrity is always an inner process where outcomes are not preordained. A person who lives by a standard of integrity will encounter setbacks in one way or another and will often have to accept the reality of small successes rather than overarching triumphs. The Celtics were just as much a model of small successes and compromises as they were of memorable victories and championships. The prisms through which light was cast in each individual player produced many different colors, and to be sure, only one of those colors was Celtic green.

So what can be done to incorporate personal integrity into a daily life practice? How can you make this part of a winning strategy, perhaps even making it part of a team effort? Let us suppose that making sound choices on your own behalf is something you have struggled with, where you have drifted into a situation where others are somehow calling the shots for you. Step back, take that in, first see what it is you want apart from what anyone else wants from you. Play a game with yourself. Imagine yourself facing the problem you are trying to deal with, the choices before you, and see yourself in a locked room with no windows or doors, no one there to advise you, reward you, or punish you for the choice you are about to make. Under those conditions, what choice would you make? Just in your head. If that choice seems impossible, ask yourself why. Keep asking questions of yourself in that closed box where no one can get at you and you will come up with answers that may surprise you even if they may not immediately solve the problem you are trying to deal with. Eventually, you will have to make a list of those answers you come up with that do not seem to jibe with what you think is called for and then, one by one, review them in your mind. Make the test of your answers how well or poorly they match the reality of your situation. Again do this in that imaginary closed room where you have no need to account to anyone but yourself. It is important for you to establish a kind of objectivity in dealing with yourself and your situation so that the choices you finally make, easy or difficult, really are in accord with that place in yourself where the buck stops, the line can't be crossed, the sense of who you are remains intact.

Let's review some Russell Rules for Integrity with a preamble: that you are the only one who can define what is and isn't right for you. It is essential that you recognize this because what you are after is the location of that place within yourself, yourself alone, that you will have to call on to choose right from wrong, wise from unwise, caring from uncaring or indifferent. With that in mind:

RUSSELL RULES

Rule One: Take responsibility for everything you do. One great quality that leaders have is the ability to take responsibility— we all know that responsibility ultimately gravitates to the person who can shoulder it. We must all be strong enough. The more you stand behind what you do or what you decide, the more you will be able to feel that is a reflection of yourself. It is your integrity that is at stake when you genuinely take responsibility for what you do.

Rule Two: Make clear choices and stand behind those choices. This rule involves utilizing three powerful words: ask, listen, decide.

Rule Three: Be fully present in whatever you are doing. Once you commit yourself to an activity, an appointment, a relationship, you have committed yourself to being there in an active and engaged way. Integrity means consciously committing yourself to reality, to what is right under your nose. It means immersing yourself wholeheartedly in whatever you are doing. Committing yourself to reality means doing everything you can to eliminate comparisons, fantasizing, wishing, or all the other mental distractions that not only take you out of the moment but also rob you of your own power. That will no doubt mean that someone else's "excellent" will, often, for you, only seem "very good." But the difference, in the end, will be about winning—and you, most of all, will be conscious of that.

Above all, integrity is your guide. If you tune in to it, it will never let you down. It will lead you through the wilderness, to beauty, hardship, difficulty, disappointment, and triumph— with the energy that is in that single light before it ever hits that prism. Above all, it will permit you to act and to live as a winner, no matter what your station in life.

REBOUNDING, OR HOW TO CHANGE THE FLOW OF THE GAME

M ISFORTUNE AND ADVERSITY HAPPEN. NOTHING CAN change that. The action that one takes afterward has nothing to do with the misfortune, and the action, not the misfortune, determines the direction in which to proceed. One of most irritating clichés floating around today is that we are supposed to see adversity as an opportunity. Self-help articles are constantly being published and books are written asking us to see the bad things that happen in life as special challenges, where, if only we teach ourselves how to react and use that bad stuff, we will thereby gain from it. We have even been told that what we've really been sent when things break down or fall apart is a kind of blessing, because at the end of that bad time we will be stronger and better able to handle the future. I don't buy any of it. This is nothing more than folks subscribing to the "I'm a victim" mentality.

Rebounding is an action taken after the other team suffers some adversity, namely, missing a shot. Or, to put it in business terms, it's capitalizing on a missed opportunity by your competition or when they don't see an opportunity. In basketball you

don't want to let your opponents have too many offensive rebounds because every offensive rebound creates another opportunity for them to score. In business you also want to block out
your opponent and be in a position to rebound. Ultimately, rebounding is about taking charge.

One of the great take-charge rebounding stories is that of
Harley-Davidson. The Harley-Davidson company for years
dominated the production of motorcycles. It was the undisputed
king of bikers the world over—until the Japanese got into
the field and nearly wiped it out. What Harley did to survive
ultimately had nothing to do with the Japanese and everything
to do with the steps it took to rebound. Some believe that the
company was bailed out by the government, which imposed
high tariffs on Japanese bikes as a way of letting Harley off the
hook. But that was not the case. The high tariffs induced Japanese firms to produce their bikes at plants in this country,
thereby doing an end around tariffs altogether.

What Harley did was to take positive actions to make the
company a winner. The first thing it did was to put a new bike
on the drawing board, one that was bigger, more comfortable
than the old models they had produced. Second, they initiated
a brilliant marketing campaign called Super-Ride, which was a
way of bringing bikers everywhere to showrooms all over the
country where they could take up a company invitation to try
out the new bikes. In just a few weekends, something like fifty
thousand bikers showed up at these showrooms to take a hog
on the road. The marketing plan also included the production
of T-shirts, sweatshirts, jackets, and other biker paraphernalia
so that when customers took advantage of a free ride on a hog,
the company was right there to exploit the opportunity that
was presented.

The turnaround—the rebound—of Harley-Davidson is one of the legendary stories of American business.

What Harley did that was so instructive was not to try in any way to "learn" from being defeated. It did not use the Japanese models that were on the market to figure out what kind of motorcycle to produce. It did not even exploit the change in tariff structures that made it much more difficult for competitors to import bikes into the United States. Instead, the company put all the bad stuff to one side, wiped the slate clean, and asked only what positive measures could be taken to make Harley-Davidson a winner in its field.

Let's put down a few working Russell Rules for becoming a winner at rebounding:

RUSSELL RULES

Rule One: Rebounding is both the end of the defense and the beginning of the offense. It is always an affirmative act and never a reaction. That you are able to rebound should always mean you are ready to take control of the situation.

Rule Two: Give up the victim mentality. Just because someone gets a shot off doesn't mean you're a bad player. Rebounding teaches us how to encapsulate an adverse moment and to move on from there.

Rule Three: Resilience is essential. Someone once said, "When you meet with triumph or disaster, treat those two impostors just the same." Resiliency, like rebounding, involves balance. One cannot win without resilience.

> *Failures and setbacks occur all the time. Each one of us deals with adversity differently. The swing of our lives from good times to bad and back again is as inevitable as variations in the weather. But in the ways we deal with these variations we define ourselves.*

Some people suffer misfortune and never really recover. Others rebound in time. Why? I've known people who have suffered the most calamitous losses only to overcome them and fully get on with their lives. They were able to do it because of rebounding and resilience.

Rebounding is the metaphor in sports I like best because it so specifically expresses my idea of consciously taking positive actions to move on. A rebound in basketball is pure, simple, isolated. It takes place in the moment, it happens, and the game moves on. Rebounding is something that can happen naturally, instinctively, but for it to be really effective it has to have an added element of conscious intent so that it can actually change the flow of the game. In the instinctive way, it can be understood as a defensive play. But in the conscious way, it should be seen as the first step of the offense.

Rebounding, for me, was a learned skill, practiced over a long period. I studied rebounding as a science. I memorized moves I thought would help me, I eliminated others that I knew would only slow me down. I watched players on offense so I would see how they reacted to the moves of centers and other defenders. I wanted to know everything I could that would enable me to make my chances of getting the rebound better. When I joined the Celtics, what I was learning was how to take the skills I had honed and adapt them to the professional game and determine which skills to use when.

> *Rebounding was my passion. Succeeding in business requires that same passion. Being a great rebounder in business requires the same brains, talent, and passion that I believe I brought to my skill at rebounding. Passion is the trigger of success. Without passion we are dormant forces and just possibilities, much like a flint awaits the iron to ignite the spark.*

To succeed you cannot play any other way than with passion. We enjoy the game more because of what we put into it. And no power is strong enough to keep us from succeeding. When I played, I never allowed myself to get distracted. Nothing happening either on the court or off could distract me from what I had to do. If the other team was having a run in their arena with the fans screaming, I did not feel any need to summon up inspiration and courage to withstand what was happening. My approach then was the same as if we were at home and ahead by twenty points. I looked at a basketball court and divided it into quadrants. Left and right below the foul circle, left and right above it. Creating this geometrical design in my mind had only one purpose: to help me better position myself for a rebound. Over time, because I was so used to doing this, it felt almost like instinct. I knew definitely that I needed to go to 1, 2, 3, or 4, depending on what kind of play was developing, who was shooting, and so forth. I didn't have to rely on extraordinary inner resources, flashes of inspiration, to tell me to get my body where it had to go. My objective was clear. I wanted to make sure of the rebound.

I knew when I first joined the Boston Celtics that I had to prove myself to my teammates on the court even though they had all been very accepting of me. In my rookie year of 1957, in my first play-off game, we played against the St. Louis Hawks. Early in the game, I missed a shot and battled for the rebound. I did not get it, and my effort sent me to the floor off the court underneath the basket. The Hawks were starting a fast break, sensing that they had an advantage because I was off the floor. Jack Coleman was leading the break and heading down the right-hand side of the court for what he thought was an uncontested layup. He was wrong. Instead of giving up and getting angry about missing my shot and not getting the rebound, I hustled back up the left-hand side of the floor immediately. By the time Jack had left his feet to lay the ball in, I had caught him. I blocked the shot and got the rebound and started our own fast break the other way. I have heard that story recounted by many of the players who saw that play. I always think of that story as a great example of resilience.

Even though I could jump as well as anyone, I knew that rebounding and shot-blocking did not really depend on how high I could jump. If I had tried to let my jumping ability be my guide, I would forever have been reacting to what was happening rather than focusing on the specific action. I remember that a few years after I retired, Red was doing a segment of

"Red on Roundball," a televised mini-clinic that used to be staged at halftime breaks in NBA games. This one was in Philadelphia, and Red invited me to participate because he wanted to demonstrate rebounding and blocking shots. I believe shot blocking is a skill similar to rebounding. Both of these skills are too often seen by coaches, players, and fans as reactive skills that can help make a defense more effective. I see these two skills being as much a part of the offense as they are a part of the defense. Bob McAdoo, a renowned scorer who was still playing then, was the guy Red had me guard. McAdoo was totally shocked that I could so easily block his shots, because this was four or five years after I was out of the game. But what he didn't understand was that I wasn't using jumping ability against him any more than I had used it when I went up against Wilt.

A rebounder, or a shot-blocker for that matter, is always at a disadvantage if he tells himself the only way he can succeed is by outjumping the guy next to him. Sometimes he will have to, but most of the time he will not. The guy who insists on going up as high as he can every time is reacting—and losing— rather than taking a specific positive action necessary to accomplish what he wants. Most of my rebounds came from positioning, where I was able to get the ball while in heavy traffic.

A good rebounder understands that he may not get all the rebounds, but he'd better try. In a game, a team will get, say, eighty-five shots at the basket; the defending team will come up with thirty-five rebounds. That means that fifty shots will have escaped the hands of the rebounder. Balls will hit the rim and bounce away from him; he will take one position but the play will somehow fail to develop as he anticipated; sometimes, another rebounder will get the better of him or a guard will strip him of the ball despite his best efforts to protect it. A rebounder has to know all this and accept it and not allow himself to get discouraged. To succeed, he has to have resilience. To have resilience means not to get distracted by the peaks and valleys in a game. This is true in business, at home, and in life. A rebound is like a crossroads. You get it, now what are you going to do with it? It's the start of a new process, one in which you have control. So the missed rebound is only a momentary event that will ultimately lead to the next shot and the rebound you don't miss. When Magic got the rebound, he'd start the break on offense himself. When Dennis Rodman got a rebound, he'd secure it, then get it off to a guard to start the offense. In both cases, as when I got a rebound, it was about starting the offense.

> **Rebounding puts you in a position to take control.**

But an important point here is that rebounding is not about returning from defeat. In my opinion, rebounding from victory is harder than rebounding from defeat.

After Cousy retired in 1963, in many people's eyes we were in trouble because he had been such a valuable asset to our championship team. Everyone thought the Celtics were now vulnerable. In 1964, we had to make the transition from Bob Cousy leading our team up the court to K.C. Jones as our floor leader. That meant an enormous change for the team because Bob and K.C. played two different games. For example, K.C.

couldn't run the fast break like Cousy. The transition game was Cousy's specialty. But K.C. was one of the greatest defensive players in history. No one could harass an opposing guard like K.C. We had to emphasize different skills to continue our winning ways. The transition of Cousy to K.C. meant we had to alter our game. Because K.C. was such a superior defensive player, I could devote more energy to offense. My assists would jump and my screens improved dramatically.

> **Regardless of our loss of Cousy, we still had to win. And one of the greatest talents of the Boston Celtics was that we could continue winning even though we had to play an entirely different kind of game.**

Winning had nothing to do with how good Cousy was, it had to do with our style of play with the players we had. That is the Celtic Pride tradition. Because Cousy and K.C. had two entirely different games, I had to determine what kind of team we would be. At that point in my career, I had been MVP three years in a row. I felt the responsibility to figure out how I would have to play differently to continue winning. Just as I had had to decide which skills to use when I got to the Celtics, now I knew I had to make adjustments. For example, Cousy led the league in assists. K.C., I knew, wouldn't. Since our potent offense was centered around passing, I had to change my game to pass more to ensure the offense kept its flow and motion.

I have been flattered when people say I always helped my

teammates play taller. What I tried to do was to make the adjustments to ensure they all could play their games better. At the end of the 1963–64 season, I was in the top ten in the league in assists. We had won another championship, and it is acknowledged that the 1963–64 Celtic team was the best ever. I agree.

The ultimate danger of being victorious is losing sight of how you got there. I have often said, "It is harder to stay a champion than it was to get there in the first place." The greatest deterrent to not repeating is always internal. Often, teams fail to prepare themselves for the season following a championship. It is hard to pinpoint the breakdown. A guy retires, a rookie makes the team, a new coach comes in, all these things change the flow. It can be a mental loss of focus, failing to report to training camp in shape, or being unable to internalize that year's success and allowing it to become a cancer eating at the team ego. Teams go from being a front-court-strong team with a change in personnel the next year into being a back-court-strong team. That change affects the team's performance. Another factor is ambition. To win year after year, all players have to be ambitious. Everyone wants to improve from year to year, but in trying to improve, players change their game, which can disrupt the balance of the team.

Rebounding from both victory and defeat requires a great deal of self-knowledge, but I think rebounding from victory is much harder. Any sales executive who is responsible for motivating his or her sales team year in and year out faces this challenge. He or she has to fight against the pressures of salespeople feeling that winning is a continuum or a gift instead of a seeing it as a reward that was fought for and gained. Over and over I have seen games where self-congratulatory lapses in commitment have resulted in the opponent scoring three or four baskets in a row before anyone realizes the opponent is now closer to winning the game.

To me, knowing how to act is everything. You cannot just throw yourself at a problem and expect to succeed. You cannot win the NBA championship on the first day of the season. It has to be won at every practice, every meeting, each and every game on the schedule. During the season, you learn to master all the important skills needed to get you to the championship game.

Adversity is said to bring out the best in people. I don't believe that for a moment. It brings out only what they have to do. It begins with self-acceptance and then proceeds, through resilience, to taking the necessary positive actions. My friend Elgin Baylor severely injured his knee in the 1961–62 season. He was out for the better part of a year. I talked to him through that period and I know how difficult it was for him. He had to go through the sort of physical rehabilitation that had commentators at the time calling him heroic. He never saw it that way. In his mind, he was a basketball player who wanted to play basketball. To do that he had to persevere in a program of exercises and reconditioning so that he could play again. For him to have focused on anything other than the daily and painfully uncertain regimen he went through would have been self-defeating. What he did was confined and limited. Each day, over many months, he had a required set of tasks to perform. In the beginning, those tasks would have seemed easy to a child—though they were as difficult for Elgin as scaling mountain peaks. He could not speed up the process. He could go to the next stage of his rehabilitation only after he had completed the prior one. There was no skipping stages, no time for wishing things were different or for feeling that the effort was somehow transforming and inspiring. It wasn't. It was perspiration, perspiration, and more perspiration. And the end result was that this very talented professional ballplayer was once again able to work. But each small action he took, each painful but positive step in the rehabilitation, was consciously undertaken. Each of those resilient actions brought Elgin Baylor closer to returning to the team with all of its important implications.

There are even more profound examples of rebounding and resilience. Think of folks like Lance Armstrong, who overcame testicular cancer to win the Tour de France in 1999 and in 2000, or Christopher Reeve, the actor who has battled against his paralysis. The actions they have taken on their own behalf are what have enabled them to make their lives into positive statements. Those who choose to dwell on the nature of their misfortune only prolong it, give it more life, allow it to define whatever afterlife it will have.

I also find situations where things have not yet been worked out, where the actions required have not yet been taken or are only just being taken, where the flow has not yet changed but where you can see process itself at work. In 2001, any number of small companies, dot-com companies, and start-up companies are in precarious shape. Some, depending on their skills in rebounding, may yet become powerful forces in their field. I have seen older companies in exactly the same position as some of these newer companies—companies like Apple or MCI—that seemed too small and overmatched to survive but that did because of their skills and resourcefulness.

The actions taken are all that matters. Some of those actions will be helpful, others will not, but it is always important to act rather than react. The determination to see through the process of team-building is everything. What is essential in every company, organization, or team is a knowledge of your business. Skill, not luck, is what is demanded. For it to be effective, action must have this multisided character to it that includes dogged persistence, a willingness to absorb information and to apply that information to oneself. Then there must be skill. The sports cliché that you need to give 110 percent is just so much hot air. Intelligence, resourcefulness, patience, and skill matter far more. By all means work hard, but don't confuse perspiration with accomplishment. There may be sweat in success, but success doesn't have sweat glands.

What we tell ourselves about misfortune is probably more important than misfortune itself. I grew up in a family that by any standard could have had more. But the word poor itself was never used in my home. A favorite saying of my father was that we were "broke, not poor."

My father understood how to change the flow of the game as well as anyone I have ever known. After he left that job he had in Louisiana and finally wound up bringing the rest of us out to Oakland, we were stuck for a place to live. Because we were broke, we couldn't afford an apartment. For the first four months, we rented an apartment above a garage. My father never thought of the misfortune that had befallen him and his family—only what he could do about it.

Finding a place seemed impossible. It was during the war, with full employment and a housing shortage. He went to the Oakland City Housing Authority and applied for an apartment in one of the projects. He was turned down. His name was put on a waiting list, and he was told to check back from time to time to see what was happening. Well, my father stopped off at the Oakland City Housing Authority to check on his application every day for four months until an apartment opened up. My father did what he had to do, a day at a time, to accomplish a goal. The real secret of his success, the way he changed the flow of the game, was his focus on small, single actions he needed to take. He knew what he wanted. But he never allowed himself to think beyond what he had to do in the moment. He got up in the morning and his only objective was to make sure he stopped off at the housing office on his way to work, to ask if that apartment had opened up yet. If he was turned down, that meant to him that he had to return the following day—something, I suspect, that made an impression on the decision-makers he was dealing with.

In what ways can rebounding work for you? How can you change the flow of the game in your life? Russell's Rules for Rebounding are here to help you do that. Let's review:

RUSSELL RULES

Rule One: Rebounding is an affirmative act. It begins the offense. The simple fact that you are in the game, able to rebound, is the first step to taking control.

Rule Two: You cannot rebound well if you have a victim mentality. If you are not the person who is called upon to shoot the game-winning shot at the end of the game, then put yourself in a position to get the rebound in case the shot is missed.

Rule Three: Build resilience both as a winner and in defeat. Understand why you are winning and never take it for granted. Recognize that it is harder to rebound from a win than to rebound from a defeat.

The governing rule of rebounding, Russell's Command-ment, is one to memorize, memorialize, and actualize:

Take control.

IMAGINATION, OR SEEING THE UNSEEABLE

I T HAS BEEN SAID THAT IMAGINATION IS MORE IMPORTANT than knowledge. Curiosity, as I have suggested, is the mother of imagination. But imagination is the father of innovation. Imagination lets you see what is possible beyond the boundaries of the basketball court, the boardroom, or the showroom floor. The only limitation is your imagination.

I am known as an innovator. I used my imagination to create innovations that I had not seen from anyone else. Even when fans claimed I was inventing new aspects of the game, I wasn't conscious of those achievements. I was simply trying to win using all the skills I had.

Prior to the time K.C. and I played at the University of San Francisco, innovation in basketball invariably had to do with offense. We tried to focus on imagining a new way to defend the basket as much as we imagined new ways to get to the basket and score. What we fundamentally changed was the idea that defense was reactive. We turned defense into an important positive transition of the game. In making defense the starting point of our offense, though I don't think we realized it at the time, we changed the tempo of the game completely. The new game we introduced became the one people recognize today.

I've shown in previous chapters some of the ways K.C. and I worked together, but our imaginitive focus on defense was special. K.C. was always trying to figure out ways to make our opponents take shots that we wanted them to take, from the spot where we wanted the shot taken, and when we were set up to do the most with the rebound. Sometimes K.C. would back his opponent to a spot beyond his normal shooting range. As his man missed his shot because he was out of his range, K.C. would get himself in position, knowing that I was ready to get the rebound and pass the ball to him for the start of a fast break. All of these concepts are not just about basketball but about innovation and competition itself.

Imagination and innovation in my life really began in my freshman year of college. I imagined things that no one else

Beginning in my freshman year, I developed the concept of horizontal and vertical games. I made a distinction between the two that others had not done. The horizontal game meant how I played side to side. The vertical game was how I played up and down. I knew that if I could integrate the two games, our team could win. I would always be in a position to determine where the ball was and where it was going.

thought were really worth much on the basketball court because the concepts were so different from the accepted view of the sport. But I knew they were important, because they worked.

Ever since my freshman year, I have looked at the game of basketball as a vertical and horizontal game. For example, jumping is a controlled asset or skill. Sometimes I jumped to touch the top of the backboard, sometimes I hardly left my feet. I have noticed that many highlight films of me show me catching so and so from behind to block his shot and get the rebound. I am always asked how I was able to do that. The answer is in the merging of the horizontal and vertical games.

It all starts with imagination. As a player with the ball moved down the court, I visualized the angle that I would need to block his shot. Then, trailing him, I would take a step to the left so that I would then be coming at the shooter from an angle, allowing me to block his shot with my left hand while landing to the player's side rather than on his back. Not only did it turn out to be an intimidating move, but by arriving on the opposite side from where I'd blocked the shot, what I had done might even have seemed a little mystical. Conversely, if the player was going down the opposite side, I'd block with my right hand and wind up on his left. By blocking shots without fouling I forced the opposition to react to the defense. Before I started to do this, the opposite was true. From that point forward, this would also help me in a practical way, because I would always be in their psyche, blocking shots I might physically never have been able to get to.

In the end, imagination and creative thinking are simply the realization that there is no particular virtue in doing things the way they have always been done. No team in basketball had become dominant until we brought our innovations to the game. Think about basketball since the Celtics of 1956–69. Few have changed the game, and those who did, did it with imagination. You can add Magic Johnson to the list of innovators because of the way he used his great size and mobility as a guard in changing some of the dynamics of offense.

How, then, do you engage the power of imagination in ways that can be practical and useful? Here are Russell's Rules for the uses and exploitation of imagination:

RUSSELL RULES

Rule One: It began when we used to stare out the window of our elementary-school classroom and think, "What if . . . ?" Imagination is a way of applying innovation and seeing a positive rather than a negative. It's better to light a candle than curse the darkness.

Rule Two: An idea can be a feat of association. Good ideas are more often the stringing together of experiences, observations, and thoughts in a way that no one has done before. Good ideas make great conclusions.

Rule Three: Visualization is a practical skill that can be sharpened through exercise. Seeing yourself and others in your "game" brings not only a familiarity, but also the ability to see past the obvious to the nuance that can be the difference between winning and not winning. Visualization puts your imagination to work. I have found that this still is critical to winning.

When we think of innovation we almost always have to recognize the power of imagination. Seeing all possibilies, seeing all that can be done, even if it has never been achieved, marks the power of imagination. There have been many great expressions of the power of imagination, but my friend Muhammad Ali may have said it best when he captured the importance of imagination with: "The man who has no imagination, has no wings." In our business of basketball, or in any business, achieving excellence has a great deal to do with taking your game to another level beyond where it is currently being played because greatness cannot come from the present, it must come from a level where no one has ventured. I'm a great *Star Trek* fan, a real Trekkie. I sometimes ask myself why I like this show so much. I think, in a large part, it has to do with *Star Trek*'s being a futuristic morality play and I enjoy the dynamics of that, but it's also the imagination of the writers and producers that never fails to stimulate me. Can you imagine the fun the early producers and writers must have had with that show? But that same opportunity faces us every day. Just like them, my innovations came from first asking "Why?" and then thinking "Why not?"

Earlier we talked about the power of curiosity, particularly as it relates to commitment. Here, let's look at curiosity not as something only the young have, but as the opportunity of adulthood. Imagination grows with use. Great imagination and innovation become more powerful as we get older. As I've always seen it, the challenge for most people is building a bridge between the shore of imagination and the shore of innovation. I remember when I was growing up adults would always say, don't cross that bridge until you come to it. But the world of innovation was created by those who in fact bravely crossed the bridge in their imaginations far ahead of the crowd.

Someone once said, first comes thought, then the organization of those thoughts into ideas and plans, and finally the transformation of those plans into reality. The beginning, though, is your imagination. I've always treated my imagination as my own private laboratory. Here is where I rehearsed the possiblities; mapped out plans, moves, and countermoves; and visualized overcoming obstacles. It was a safe and successful place where imagination turned possibility into reality.

The free-floating kind of imagination that we all have, that doesn't necessarily result in a company, product, or innovation, is still a potent power.

Human beings dream. They see things that were never seen before. The images that seemingly just appear in our minds out of nowhere are as much a part of how we live our lives as drawing breath. It is therefore just as certain that many of the products of imagination will go nowhere, will dissipate like wisps of morning fog when the sun comes out.

> *But imagination has this unexpected aspect of actualization built into it. What we see in our dreams or fantasies can often be made real when we then commit resources, labor, ingenuity, effort, to back it up. That is precisely the task of enlightened leadership.*

We begin any understanding of imagination with an ultimate respect we pay to dreamers, to those who see things that never were when they close their eyes and then say, "Why not?"

Artists are the ones we almost always associate with imagination. And perhaps there is no better place to start a discussion of our rules than with a reminder of just what imagination means to artists. Artists have visions. They see things that never were. Images, symbols, representations of the most fantastic shapes, ideas, concepts, come to mind. And then something else happens. The images, the mental representations, become actualized in paintings, stories, poems, tapestries, pieces of music, buildings. Writers for centuries imagined the existence of heaven and hell. They wrote about it as though it actually existed. The great Italian poet Dante closed his eyes and imagined heaven and hell in ways described in the Bible. There were layers upon layers of each realm, rings upon rings, there was a geography almost as exact as that which humans relied upon to navigate the known globe. Dante then converted what he saw in his imagination into one of our greatest literary treasures. The poem he created was real and will be with us forever. He actualized what he had seen in his imagination.

Great painters and sculptors do this all the time. They see what was never before seen and then actualize the products of their imagination in works of art. But so do scientists, inventors, builders, manufacturers, people in every walk of life. Imagination only begins with the dream. Innovation then occurs through actualization.

I used imagination in my life from as far back as I can remember. In the South, in those early years, I loved listening to the stories my aunts, uncles, and grandparents told. I would dream about them when I went out to play, and I would make up some of my own. When I was older and I was living in California and I was spending a lot of time in the library, the love I developed for painting made me use my imagination in a more practical way. I wanted to produce the same things great artists had produced. Transferring images from Michelangelo and Leonardo to my brain, I held them there until I was sure I saw each line, each shape, so perfectly I could then pick up a pencil and transfer those images to blank paper. My goal of actualization was to make Michelangelo's work my work. I did this diligently enough to see that I could use my mind in that way, that is, that I could transfer pictures in my brain into something actual, something more than mere appreciation.

I have already mentioned how I used the same sort of approach I had taken to those great painters to basketball players I admired. But this process, I realize now, was a little more complicated and involved more than merely reproducing the contents of someone else's imagination. With the old masters, my goal was to do what they did. When I began "imagining" the moves of those two basketball players I so greatly admired on that early pre-college tour I took to Canada, my goal was never to reproduce what they did—but to counter their moves. I closed my eyes and saw each move that Bill Treu and Eural McKelvey made. For a long time, I thought what I was doing was trying to find a way to copy them. Each of these players did things I admired. Treu was a terrific shooter with great moves, but he eventually chose a life with the Mormon Church over basketball, so he never played in the NBA. I loved the way he moved as a guard—he was Earl Monroe at three-quarter speed. His footwork, his hand speed, the way he was able to free himself in traffic to get off a shot—all of that burned onto my brain like a motion picture film so that I would deliberately set time aside on that trip (in my hotel room, riding along on the bus) to just close my eyes and let the images flow. Then, when we had practice or a game, I'd see how much I could incorporate.

With McKelvey, who had remained a lifelong friend, it was a little different. McKelvey was an outstanding rebounder who understood postitioning and timing. I was enormously helped by visualizing his moves, but again I was constrained because what I was really doing was imitating, not creating.

What changed things for me, what made this imaginative process creative, was when I began to see in my mind's eye the moves I would need to defend against these players. Each move I then came up with was an invention of mine, something that had not existed before. I watched the way Treu threw the weight of his body one way, shifted by using short, quick steps, then projected his body in a completely different direction. So he could, in an instant, free himself for a shot.

I saw the moves defenders had to make to stop that move of his. I was able to see my body leaning slightly into the player but keeping my weight back. I could see the way my feet would move in longer strides but always in a flexed position so that I could recover from any fake faster than the player who did the faking would ever imagine. I saw myself able to let a player like Treu, with his brilliant moves, step past me, but then I saw how I would be able to surprise him totally by catching him from behind.

With McKelvey the process was the same. I watched his moves as a defender, someone who knew how to clear the boards and start his team going on offense. I watched the way he measured angles, calculated the geometry of balls hitting off the backboard and rim, and I devised my own calculations that would take away the advantage a skilled player like that had. I created defense in the center position so that I could keep up with players as speedy and mobile as a guard, as well-positioned and intelligent as a resourceful rebounder.

At that time, just before I was starting my college career, I quite consciously began using my imagination in a way that allowed me to apply what hadn't been seen before. I began systematically inventing another kind of game from the essentially flat-footed one I had grown up with.

When I got to the Celtics, I knew that I was doing things differently from other centers and big men. I kept seeing things other players did not and translating them into moves I could make that were all my own. I clearly understood something I had put together as a concept back when I was a freshman in college thinking about the horizontal and vertical games. The game up to that point was known as vertical. The rim was an object above the heads of the players, the purpose of the game was to get the ball from down below through the rim up above. Players, whether they were dribbling the ball, shooting the ball, rebounding the ball, or whether they told themselves or not, all thought that the object was to score or to control the ball until it was possible to score. One of the college teams of that era operated with a slow-down system that resulted in final scores that read like baseball scores. But even there, the objective was the same—to stay in control of that vertical line between the ball, the player on the floor, and the basket.

What I saw was how much more there was to the game than that. I would lie awake at night and play with numbers. How much time was there in an NBA game? Forty-eight minutes. How many shots were taken in a game? Maybe a hundred and sixty, eighty or so on each side. I calculated the number of seconds each shot took—a second, a second and a half—and then I multiplied by a hundred. Two hundred forty seconds at most—or four minutes. Then add a single extra second for a foul shot missed and then the ball put in play; add another minute at the most. So, five minutes out of forty-eight are actually taken up in the vertical game. What happens during the rest of the game? That was the challenge to my imagination.

My competition with Wilt fed my imagination as nothing else. He was devastating vertically, but I had an advantage horizontally. In a forty-eight-minute game I tried to get him to play thirty minutes or more horizontally. The more I could get him horizontal, the greater our chance of winning. But part of the hell I had to go through was playing his vertical game while trying to get him to play my horizontal one. I was constantly trying to entice him. I'd make as many moves side to side as possible to force him to move side to side. Everyone knew his favorite shot was a fadeaway jump shot, so I leaned at him in a way to force him back from were he was comfortable, causing him to be out of his comfort zone. Because he knew I could block his in-close fadeaway shot, he began innovating by fading away farther out from the basket. Some nights he'd get so annoyed with what was going on he'd just say the heck with the fadeaway and he'd start dunking on me. And those I couldn't block for fear of losing an arm.

The additional problem in playing Wilt was that unlike Treu and McKelvey, whom I could watch from the sideline, with Wilt it was a constant work in progress. This meant visualizing from the floor because that was where I was playing him. I would always try to position myself to force him to take the shot I wanted him to take. This didn't always work because he was so good, and it would be unrealistic to believe it could.

Of course, my goal in this visualization was to teach myself how best to play him, but I was also filling in the blanks of the game I had innovated. I saw endless creative possibilities of defense that had just not been in the game before, the particular ways quickness created unimagined opportunities.

> *Visualizing what I needed to do against Wilt opened up so many moves for me. Because I could not challenge him directly, I had discovered new ways to defend him and other big men. I began to measure the court in a geometric way, understanding what kind of shots were most likely to be taken from what part of the floor. Nudging a player toward an area, I knew the most likely shot to be taken—and therefore I knew what I would need to do to defend against it.*

I have been asked many times how I would play against some of the NBA's greatest centers, men whom I never had the chance to compete against. Here again, they got the question backward. But putting that aside, I know how to play all the great players because I have already played them in my imagination. Let me explain how I would have played against one of the all-time great centers, Kareem Abdul-Jabbar. My strategy would begin by making him run the floor on defense. For starters, this would change his game because he would be expending much more energy. Because he was right-handed and I was left-handed and the key to defense is footwork, I could slide along his stomach and get to his sky hook with my left hand. You could never defend Kareem by reacting to what he did. If he started his move, it would be too late to do much about it. Defending Kareem began when he crossed the center-court line. If he was going to his spot on the right side, I'd get there first. If he was going to his spot on the left side, I'd get there first. Most guys have a spot they like to start from, and nothing annoys them more than to see you there first, waiting for them. When I played Wilt, he used to get so annoyed when I would get to his spot because it meant he had to move me off his spot to start his game. This would be an effective way of creating a diversion to distract him out of his game. Since I never played against Kareem, I don't know how good his ears were. This would be important because a big part of my game was conversation. I would have searched until I found out what would distract him and then determined what the impact of that distraction was. Sometimes if you really got someone annoyed, he'd play better than if he wasn't annoyed.

The last game of my career was the seventh and final game for the NBA Championship against the Lakers in Los Angeles. We were not supposed to win. Everyone considered them the stronger team, and when we got to L.A., the outcome was predetermined. The Lakers had planned the entire scenario for the championship celebration that would follow after the final buzzer. Ten thousand balloons, in a huge net in the ceiling of the Forum, would be released. After the game the USC band would come out on the floor and play "Happy Days Are Here

Again." The champagne was on ice, and Jerry West, Elgin, and Wilt would come out to center court for interviews and all the pomp and circumstance that surrounds a championship won on a home court.

I did something then I had never before done in my entire career. When I walked into the locker room that night, I realized I needed an innovative way to get my team to a level they might not otherwise have been at. A level necessary to win that specific night against that specific team. I showed them the Lakers' victory program, which outlined step-by-step what the Lakers' postgame victory would look like, and told them there was no way in my wildest imagination I could see the Lakers winning. The plan was simple. We were going to run them into the ground. We were capable of playing a variety of different games. Innovation for us was simple. We could run with anyone. Changing our style that night wasn't hard since we'd played it before. They hadn't seen it and wouldn't be able to make the adjustments. And we ran and ran, leading by seventeen points at halftime and, in the end, winning our eleventh championship.

A year ago, I met John Glenn. I was sitting next to him at dinner and he complimented me on a great career.

I thanked him and said, "Looking at your career, though, I don't think I would have allowed them to strap me to a rocket and light it!"

"That was fairly routine," he replied.

"Oh, another day at the office?" I said.

"It wasn't quite like that. It was part of a process." He told me space travel was something he had envisioned as a pilot, and he had always been a pilot. It wasn't a big deal, he said, because he had been flying since he was in his twenties. He had been preparing for that moment of liftoff for years, he said. He had been a pilot in World War II, he had been a test pilot, he had been working in the space program for a long while. His inspiration had really occurred years before, when he had first taken up flying. Everything after that was putting into practice what he had first dreamed about. The actual experience of space travel, he said, was a bit more than a day at the office, but it represented a step-by-step undertaking where what was a spectacular, inspired individual moment to everyone else was really part of an effort that had begun with a moment of imagination and had since been transformed by his immersion in what he called a team effort.

> *The Celtic teams I played for were collections of not only great basketball players but highly creative individuals, drawing on knowledge and skills to accomplish a team goal of winning championships. Imagination for us—because we were a team—was always the result of both actualization and organization.*

We as Celtics supported each other, watched each other, incorporated into our individual imaginations the thinking, the practice, of others. We were able to visualize for each other as, perhaps, we might not have been able to left just to ourselves.

In 1968, when Philadelphia had us on the brink of elimination in the play-offs, we had a two-point lead with twelve seconds left, and I was fouled. If I made one of the two free throws, we would ice the game (there was no three-point shot back then). If I missed both shots, Philly would have a last shot to tie, to take us into overtime—and perhaps close us out. I stepped to the line and missed my first free throw. At that point, Sam Jones walked over to me, and after he talked to me, I made the next shot. We won.

Later, in the locker room, writers crowded around wanting to know what Sam had said to me, whether it was encouraging or inspirational. When I shot fouls successfully, I always flexed my knees. When I missed, I was most often stiff-legged. "Flex your knees, Bill," was the inspirational word I got from him at that last, crucial moment. It was about as inspiring as a car manual, but it was the only thing I needed to hear at that moment for us to win. Do not confuse imagination with inspiration. The Celtics won infinitely more games because of the power of imagination than because of inspirational talks and speeches.

Here is a review of the Russell Rules on imagination and leadership that can get you and your team into whatever championship game you are striving to win:

RUSSELL RULES

Rule One: Look for the positive in your imagination. If you go into a dark room, find the light switch.

Rule Two: Creative imagination means an idea is a feat of association. Taking unrelated thoughts or ideas and stringing them together sometimes creates a whole new concept. It creates order out of chaos.

Rule Three: Practice visualization. Try to run through scenarios or situations before you experience them so that when you do experience them, it is familiar to you. Actualize your imagination.

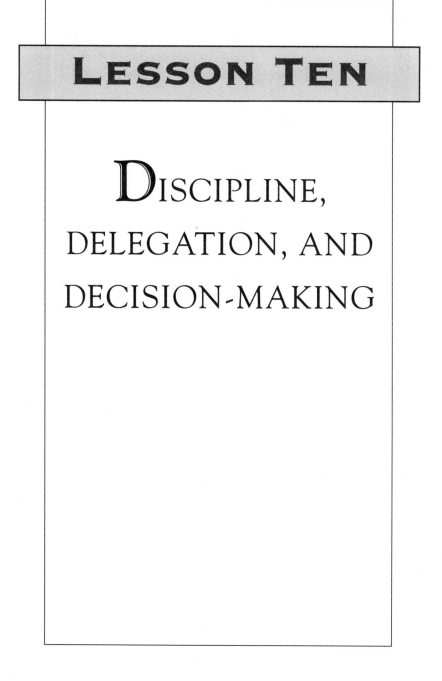

DISCIPLINE, DELEGATION, AND DECISION-MAKING

DECISION-MAKING IS CENTERED AROUND GATHERING IN-formation, assessing it, and deciding what is pertinent for your specific situation, and what is the right decision for that moment. It may not work out, but knowing that you made the most informed, thoughtful, and intelligent decision based on the information you could gather at the time is all that you can hope for.

Leadership is deciding when and where to implement the decision.

What all sound decision-making has in common is discipline. Whether one chooses to let others in on the decision-making or not, discipline is required because any choice means that competing possibilities exist and therefore attractive alternatives or seemingly easier ways must be resisted. When decision-making is really sound, that sense of competing interests is likely to be strongest and will thus demand from a leader an ability to remain focused no matter what.

So what are we to make of this most fundamental yet

many-sided aspect of leadership? Here are the Russell Rules to help us take the right action:

RUSSELL RULES

Rule One: All choices must be with a clear and attainable goal in mind, even if it is only to move the process from point A to point B in an alphabet of points before success is assured. Decisions made without clear goals in mind are likely to create confusion, resentment, and failure. Others will quickly recognize it when goals are not spelled out, and even if there is a residue of good feeling for the decision maker, a subtle sense of uneasiness and uncertainty will tend to be undermining.

Rule Two: Delegating authority in decision-making can only take place successfully when there is absolute confidence in those to whom power is given. In delegating, the process is always about teamwork, not about surrendering responsibility. The goal in delegating is to make the team better, whether it is a corporation, a university, or a family. The CEO, the head of the family, the president, or whoever still has to be responsible for the choices to be made. They will be made in his or her name, and he or she will have to stand behind them. Therefore, in delegating, you must do everything possible to remain in active touch with those to whom power has been given. Make delegating a process of communication rather than the giving up of anything.

Rule Three: Think everything through first, then stick your neck out. Making no decision is far more dangerous than making the wrong decision. Just look at how the Celtics made decisions on what plays to use against a specific team.

The most important, if most obvious, aspect of decision-making is having clear goals in mind. On the Celtics the clear goal was winning championships. Our CEO, Walter Brown, delegated responsibility for those basketball decisions that were essential for team-building to Red Auerbach. Red, in turn, delegated much of his authority to his players, whom he trusted profoundly.

Red's choices were always clear. He had ultimate responsibility for filling our roster. Therefore, he had to decide which players would be most likely to advance the goal of winning championships. To begin with, he had a standard he used that helped him make his choices. Did the player he was considering bringing to his team already know about winning? Did he come from a winning program? Did he understand that winning was expected, not just something to be hoped for? But it went beyond the important criterion of being a "practiced winner"; being selected to be a Celtic had as much do to with Red's belief that you as a player could be entrusted with the culture of Celtic Pride. Could you be trusted to demonstrate curiosity, commitment, team ego, active listening skills, integrity, selflessness? Could you be entrusted with the responsibility that Red would delegate to you? What about your team?

Sam Jones was the surprise pick in the 1957 draft, the Celtics' number one choice and the eighth overall. Writers, even scouts, had never heard of North Carolina Central College. But somehow Red had. He knew that North Carolina Central had a winning program, but he had never seen Sam play. Because Red trusted his players, he had asked a former player, Bones McKinney, who was coaching at Wake Forest, who the best players were in the SEC. Bones said, the best player in the South is Sam Jones. So Red, with his trust of his players, took Bones's word for it without ever seeing Sam play.

From the beginning it was clear to Red that Sam was an incredible offensive player. But what Red and the rest of us also quickly learned was that Sam was more than an adequate defensive player; when he put his mind to it, he was a great defensive player.

In 1973, after I'd left the game, I visited Red at Milbrook, the basketball camp he ran during the summers. At that time, the Celtic team was in transition. Red was not quite sure where things were headed. He had a player in camp, Dave Cowens, whom he liked and thought of as a forward. When he pointed him out, I could see why. Red said, "I've got a good one here, but I need a center."

"You have a center," I said to him immediately.

"Where?" said Red. He looked at me and I pointed to Cowens.

"You got one there. The redhead. He's your center."

Red said he didn't think Cowens was tall enough, though he was as tall as I was. Use him in the high post, I said, he'll do all you want him to. The guys he can't guard can't guard him.

> *Red was always relying on us to get the job done because he trusted not only our talent but our intelligence. In delegating, he empowered us. He made us co-coaches, even though ultimate responsibility always rested with him.*

Big men won't be able to guard him because he'll be too quick for them. Red thought about it for a second and agreed.

How did Red help me develop the skills of decision-making as a coach? I think I learned a lot from having to coach the team after Red got thrown out of games. I believe that Red got thrown out of more games than any other coach in the history of the NBA. In 1966 alone, his final year, he got thrown out of twenty-two games, including the All-Star game. I am not suggesting that he did this intentionally for my benefit, though there was one, because I had coached twenty-two games before I ever started officially coaching. This confirmed to me that I could be a player-coach.

In retrospect, I think two factors contributed to his finding the dressing room before we did. First, he had announced his retirement from coaching before the season and the referees weren't cutting him any slack. He was always in their faces and they weren't going to let it slide in the '65–66 season. Red had more passion for winning than almost anyone else I've ever known, and he used his words to inspire, incite, and ignite. Secondly, if we needed to be motivated, his getting thrown out of the game always did it. For example, we'd not be playing well and he'd get thrown out of a game. We automatically felt that the referees were attacking us personally as a unit and we'd step up to show them. It was going to take more than that to beat us. Since we couldn't beat on the refs, we'd focus on the other team. We'd find any excuse to win!

Red's leadership style was interesting in that he was a volatile, emotional man who might easily have been a dictator but who wasn't. Red never hid who he was. You always knew where he stood, what he felt. His temper was quick, but his intelligence was even quicker. When Red got on a player's back, he did not focus attention on that one player. He never embarrassed him in front of his teammates. Instead, he would light into all of us. He'd rant and rave about "You guys aren't keeping your eyes open" or "You guys could have blocked out but you didn't" or "How come you guys won't set a pick when you know that's what the play calls for, whatsamatter with you guys?" It was perfect. No one liked being yelled at, but everyone accepted the way Red did it because we all understood what he was doing. The team. The team. The team. You couldn't forget that in even the smallest decisions he made—and that we made.

In my final season with the team, we were not expected to win another championship. We had finished fourth in the Eastern Division. As player-coach, I carefully reviewed the season in my mind, trying to figure out what might have been the problem. I knew who our opponents were (physically, emotionally, and psychologically), how they played in every situation, what we could expect—just as they knew who we were and what we did. When I looked at a game-by-game breakdown of our season, however, I noticed something curious. We lost seventeen games by three or fewer points. That meant, to me, that we were not closing well. We did not really have a last-second shot play that was effective in putting us ahead. I had a decision to make.

In practice, when I called the guys together I told them what I had found and that we needed to come up with a last-second shot play. Now, I remembered quite vividly what Red had gone through when he had made the decision to introduce a "new" play to us years ago. My decision was a little different. I left it to the guys to come up with the play. My decision, in essence, was to delegate, enroll the team in the solution and then let the players implement their decision which would really be mine.

There were several factors involved. The first, of course, was a willingness to let others, my players, carry the weight of this decision with me. The decision, therefore, from the start was outside-in, coming from the team. Second, a new play meant breaking the Celtic mold. Because we had relied on the same six plays for so long and had been so committed to them as a means to our success, any deviation now was risky. I was also most wary of "last minute" plays but I knew we needed one.

The way I implemented my decision that day in practice was to tell my players what I was looking for and then ask them what plays they had used in college at the end that had been especially successful. John Havlicek and Larry Sigfried were from Ohio State and had what I thought to be the best play.

When we first ran the play, it took twenty-seven seconds to run. Obviously, it would never do in the final seconds of a game. We had to do better. Every one on the team understood this. Our mission—collectively and individually—became clear. To implement the decision to run a buzzer-beating play, every guy on the floor had to do his utmost to make it work. It could not be the work of a single player, no matter how talented he was. It had to be the work of a team. We were in the play-offs, the goal was winning a championship. Each individual player had to find in himself what he could do to cut the time of that play down. He had to take into account what his teammates did. He had to be mindful of every move made by everyone else. The only thing that mattered was whittling that play down to a point where we could use it at the end of a game.

When we finally were ready, we were able to run that play in four seconds.

We had taken twenty-three seconds out of it by devoting ourselves to a solution. We ran the play in the play-offs and won five of our games en route to our championship by three points or less. The decision—which involved delegation, risk, commitment, discipline and responsibiblity—was, to me, the epitome of what sound decision-making is all about.

There is a theory that I described in lesson four that describes two very different ways in which leadership decisions are made. One of these ways I like to call inside-out, the other outside-in. An inside-out leader or decision maker looks at the world from the perspective of his or her own needs. The decision has little to do with the needs of the audience or customer . . . it's fundamentally I have this, or I need this, and I'm going to make a decision on those needs. The leader or decision maker sees everything from his or her own perspective. She takes her cues, her points of departure, her objectives, from herself, from the ultimate source: her own talents and abilities. She sees the world with herself at the center (whether she means to think that way or not). Decision-making, responsibility, accountability, everything must come from her because she is the source, the font of authority and wisdom. Of course, any viewpoint that begins with you as the center of the universe, the repository of all talent and responsibility, is bound to be narrow, self-oriented, and narcissistic.

On the other hand, an outside-in decision-making style focuses on the needs of the audience. What's important to them? It is an inclusive view of problem-solving or resolution. In fact, it is an inclusive sales strategy because it takes in the needs of the customer and then allows the seller to "merge" the needs of the buyer with the wishes or attributes of the seller. Most effective outside-in thinkers are also effective listeners. Think back to lesson four, on creating your leadership style, and lesson three, on listening: these are all important aspects to making the right decision. Active listening allows you to hear what isn't being said as much as what is being said. Becoming an outside-in thinker requires a deep understanding of the needs of the "buyer." I don't know a more effective way to get that obvious and hidden understanding than to listen. Which type of manager are you? Which type of team player are you? Which type of decision maker are you? Inside-out and exclusive or outside-in and inclusive?

When you think about it, those are the two ways that Wilt and I were very different. Wilt, and justifiably so, recognized that he was an enormous talent. Quite literally an enormous talent. And he felt that if he went out every night and played as hard as he could, he would make his team win. He was so intense in his desire to be "the factor" and was "the man." Wilt believed that in basketball one player can have so much influence on the outcome of the game. When I played, we often had to go through his team to get to the championship. In fact, his team was the only team to break our championship streak. But it was only for one year. Conversely, my approach was more inclusive. For us to win every night, I accepted the responsibility to play well, but getting my team to have a good game would ensure more victories and I wouldn't have to work quite as hard. Getting the ball quickly to Cousy or K.C. enabled the team to move the ball upcourt for an easy shot, but it also kept me from getting more points. Did that matter? Yes, because scoring is fun. But I realized our team couldn't win if I was the center of the universe. I was the catalyst and the finisher, not the center. My battles with Wilt were a classic exclusive-versus-inclusive matchup. Or, as I like to think of it, a classic inside-out versus outside-in matchup.

> *In my opinion the outside-in decision maker is the ultimate team player because he or she also possesses one additional and vital aspect of behavior—discipline. Discipline is in part the ability to eliminate all the competing, vying personal needs and inclinations that will get in the way of making decisions that will benefit the team.*

Discipline is not really so much about self-abnegation as it is about having control of and a plan for your personal life to the point where you can do whatever you must to follow through. Individuals as much as people in collective settings are faced with this problem.

Teamwork, of course, requires the ultimate in discipline (and for me, it provides the ultimate in rewards). There will always be the temptation to do for oneself first, to fill the needs one has to be recognized, applauded, and compensated. On the Boston Celtics, teamwork was always about discipline. There was a constant tension between what individuals wanted for themselves and what they could give to their team. Although all of us wanted the same thing, we were still faced, individually, with who we were. Sam, for example, found it uncomfortable to step up to the dominating talent he had, but he did that because he knew that was called for. Scoring a ton of points was never his objective per se, only to give what he knew he had to supply for us to win.

Some decisions require most of all the ability to let go, particularly where unanticipated bad results have occurred. For individuals, teams, companies, mistaken choices are always part of the picture. How we handle these decisions is almost more important than the decisions themselves, because we need to learn from our mistakes, let go, and go on.

> **Letting go is most difficult when we are most personally attached. The decision one makes to retire comes to mind. An individual can make no more important decision, yet what is most essential in making that decision is the ability to let go. It is hard to leave a company, a team, a way of life. So much has been invested, so much history, so much experience. What is important is the ability to let go so that you can move on to the next phase of your life.**

When I retired, I did not tell anyone of my plans until I got to the end of the season. I told myself that to continue playing at the only level I would accept required I have certain strengths, and these had begun leaving me. But I knew at the end of the 1969 season, when we had beaten the Lakers for the championship, that I had played my last game. I knew that because I was sure I was not able to bring myself mentally and emotionally to the arena every night. One reason why I had agreed to become player-coach was that I had begun getting bored after winning eight straight championships. That might sound egotistical or incongruous, but it was true. In fact, one reason I didn't have an assistant coach when I was coaching the Celtics was that it kept me more focused on coaching. I had to do everything and make every decision myself. Becoming a player-coach was a perfect remedy for my drifting away mentally from our game. It still surprises me how many fans don't know that we won two championships without an assistant coach.

The day I retired is a day I will never forget. We won the championship on Tuesday night in Los Angeles. We had Wednesday off, and on Thursday Red called to tell me a reporter had just left his office. The reporter had asked Red an especially stupid question. He had said, "Are you satisfied with the coaching you had this year?"

Red was incredulous. "What are you talking about, two days ago we won the world championship."

"Yeah, but could you have had a better regular season record with a better coach?" said the reporter.

Red told me what had happened. I said, "Don't worry, Red, it doesn't make a difference because I've made my mind up to leave anyway." He was startled and asked me not to say a word to anyone, because if it had gotten out, he knew I was too stubborn to reverse my decision.

I had decided to retire before the season had begun but chose not to announce it for three reasons. First, I didn't want to go through the year with everyone saying good-bye. That would place too much attention on me. Secondly, Sam had announced that the '68–69 season was his last, and I didn't want to take anything away from the recognition he really deserved. Third, it would have changed the dynamics of my relationship with the team, and I was unwilling to take the chance.

Retiring was my final victory. Not staying a minute too long, or a season too long, let me leave on my own terms. Knowing when to retire is difficult for any athlete or businessperson. You have to give up so much and start another life. But making that decision and sticking to it is one of the most rewarding decisions you will ever make in your life. I encourage folks to look at this moment as starting a new season in a different game.

So, let's look at those Russell Rules once more. The rules on decision-making, delegation, and discipline are simple but they work:

RUSSELL RULES

Rule One: All decisions need to have a clear and attainable goal. Without that, no one will take your decision seriously or follow your directive with any passion.

Rule Two: Delegation can only become comfortable when the person you are delegating to has your full respect and confidence. You get this respect and confidence from the decisions that you make.

Rule Three: Think, then stick out your neck. Do not be afraid of making the wrong decision.

The world has become an infinitely more complex and interrelated environment, one where it has become even clearer to me that the power of making a correct decision lies within each of us and offers us always the promise of leadership and the rewards that come with it.

EVERYONE
CAN WIN

GROWING UP, I KNEW MANY PEOPLE WHOSE LIVES TAUGHT me all I needed to know about winning and leadership. I spent my early years around people who did not have material wealth or big names but who taught me everything I needed to know about winning. I learned that it did not matter what kind of job you had but what kind of work you did.

It never occurred to me at any point that failure was possible in my life because I had been raised to think that anything I did would be successful depending on my willingness to succeed, to see myself as a winner, no matter what.

For a period in my life between high school and college, I did not know what I was going to do. I was like a lot of young people today, searching for a direction. But I had a willingness to work and to learn. My goal at the time was just to earn enough money so that I could go on to college, but in the work I did at that naval shipyard, all I ever thought about was making sure that I could go home every day thinking that I had learned everything possible that day.

Winning doesn't happen automatically. It is always a

step-by-step process that means that wherever you are in life, whatever you are doing, now is the right time to begin working, this moment is exactly the right moment to begin seeing yourself as a winner.

At one point in his career, Bill Gates wasn't a colossus in the high-tech world. He was just a smart kid who had a lot of energy and a tendency to get into trouble at school. His parents sent him off to a prep school where he was introduced for the first time to the world of computers. He was fascinated. He gave himself totally to finding out everything he could about this new, cumbersome technology. He experimented, he played, and above all, he worked. No one immersed himself more thoroughly in what he was doing with, seemingly, no tangible reward awaiting him as he did. But by the time he had moved on to college and the industry itself had grown, Gates's passion began to pay off. He, and friends of his, had made themselves expert computer programmers. They became so good at what they did, their professors began to refer to their work to understand their own. Eventually, Gates translated his passion into the enormous business success he has since earned.

But what are we to make of that? What are the Russell Rules about putting yourself into a position to win?

RUSSELL RULES

Rule One: Look for an opportunity to win in any situation. Don't wait for a promotion or a better job. What I absorbed growing up and in every subsequent phase of my life was an understanding that winning was always a possibility. Don't overlook it. Ask yourself, always, what does it take to win *today?*

Rule Two: You have to be the one to determine how to measure winning. That means making sure you do not allow others to define how the game is going to be played. You have to familiarize yourself with the standards of your work. If expertise is what it takes, you have to do whatever is necessary to make yourself an expert, but it is always up to you to make sure you understand the crucial difference between doing something well or poorly. That's the real difference between winning and losing. If you are true with yourself, you will be true with everyone else, you will win no matter where you are, no matter what you are doing.

Rule Three: Start now, not tomorrow. This is essential because it means that you commit yourself wherever you find yourself. It means that if you are the twelfth man on your team, if you sit at the end of the bench, you make the most of an opportunity others would let slip.

When K.C. first came to the team, there was a lot of sniping that he was just a fill-in, hired because I pressured the team (which was never the case). In fact, it is insulting to even think that. It was not only insulting to me, but also to K.C. and Red. I would never jeopardize the success of our team for any personal relationship. In the beginning, K.C. didn't play. He was the tenth guy on our team, the last guy on the bench, the easiest guy for the media and the fans to overlook, the first player "experts" would have considered expendable. K.C. had to deal with the expectations and assumptions projected onto the guy who was last in line, who had, almost literally, been labeled and dismissed.

From the start, K.C. looked only at the opportunity that he saw in his situation. In his mind, who he was had nothing to do with his position at the end of the bench. In his first season, he didn't play in twenty-five games. It wasn't about K.C.'s talent, but about the coach's decision on the rotation of his guards. To anyone who came to a Celtics game, K.C.'s job was to stand up and listen when the team huddled on the sidelines during time-outs, and to get in line with everyone else during warm-ups and take his handful of layups.

But K.C. saw something very different. He accepted his role without complaint, then used it for all it was worth. There was never a tougher player in Celtic practices. Starters—the stars on the team—always knew they were in for it when they went up against him in practice. Bill Sharman said one day that games were easy for him after practicing against K.C.

> **K.C. may have been a tenth man, but he thought like a winner, and the way he thought about himself eventually enabled him to not only move up the ladder but also become a Hall of Fame player. He did not let his situation dictate whether he could be a winner. He chose to be a winner even when it seemed he did not have a choice in the matter.**

In my years, another player on our team was also seemingly not in a position to be a winner—John Thompson. He was a backup center for me. John was the kind of player who not only gave his best effort but was always there with his eyes and mind wide open. You knew he was learning, asking questions not only of others but of himself. At one point, before he had settled into the team, he went up against me in practice and had a relatively easy time. He told me later that he thought he would be able to do everything I did because he had essentially done that in practice. But then, when it was time to play for keeps, he saw another player—one who let him know that he would have to find a level of success for himself that was all his own. John made every minute of his professional career count. He absorbed more about the game than perhaps any other player I have known. The results in his coaching career at Georgetown have been obvious. He has coached great teams and won a national championship in 1984. John Thompson knows how to win—and even more important, he knows how to teach others to win.

When I got to the Celtics, I knew what I could do as a player, and I could also see that it was up to me to show others what I knew about myself. I was fortunate in my coach and my teammates, but I was perfectly aware that Boston had traded for me to fill a specific need. The Celtics at that point were a good team but lacked a dominating center. The label I came with said I couldn't shoot, was a poor free-throw shooter, and would generally be of little use on offense.

I knew that others thought I had problems shooting, but I knew that I could shoot the ball and score points. I therefore always made sure that I took shots I had a good chance of making. I saw myself as a multidimensional player. I played defense differently from other centers playing at that time. I knew that about myself, I knew I could cover the court. I was quick, I could put the ball on the floor, I could move left or right, away from the ball, I could handle the ball out of bounds, or even bring it up if I had to. I could set plays at the top of the key or down low. I had to define my own standard of success even though I had to answer to the team's standard of what it needed. The team, it turned out, wanted less from me than I wanted from myself. I had to incorporate what my coach wanted from me, but I owed it to him, my teammates, and to myself to use all the skills I had. When I joined the team, I did not start for the first twelve games, though I played quite a bit in all of them. But from the beginning I knew exactly what I needed to do to seize the opportunity I had, to be successful, first, in my own eyes.

Several years ago, I was at the National Mentoring Conference in Philadelphia. At a reception, a guy came up to me and said that he had run a cafeteria in 1956 at the Bunker Hill Air Force Base in Peru, Indiana, where the Olympic basketball team—of which I had been a member—had trained. The guy told me he had a signed photograph of the fifteen players on the Olympic team. And then he told me a story.

Soon after the Olympic team broke camp and began touring, a sportswriter from Chicago, who was a friend, asked him what he thought my chances would be in the pros. The guy said he told his friend that I'd never stick, I'd be cut within a year. Everyone was saying that, he said, other players, the coach. I was the sixth- or seventh-best player on the Olympic team, and they all thought I just wasn't any good. The guy shook his head: "I'm still trying to figure out what it was I did not see." I told him that in all likelihood what had happened was that he had been listening to the coaching staff and to other players. What those folks had not been able to see was that everywhere I had been as a player, my team had won. That's what I did as a basketball player. I wasn't interested in how I looked to others or how they interpreted what I said in press conferences, only in doing everything I could to help my team win basketball games—and I knew how to do that.

Coming from the background I did, I was never really surprised to see talented people have to fight to make lives for themselves. It is true that though talent, effort, and determination will enable some people to make their own way, many others fall by the wayside. People are worn down by the constant stereotyping, or else they place their dreams on hold while they deal with the more mundane needs of survival. Many talented people are held back through no fault of their own. I believe everyone can win in his or her own right and should be given that opportunity. That is why I have always supported affirmative action in our society.

I am an advocate of the program, but not for the reasons too easily assumed by critics—that it is a way of artificially and unfairly redressing imbalances of opportunity according to race. Affirmative action has always seemed to me, as public policy, a matter of enlightened self-interest. All of us stand to gain when we remove barriers that allow people to go as far as their talents and efforts can take them. On one of my lecture tours a few years ago, I was at a college and a student came up to me afterward and asked me about the issue. He thought that affirmative action might unfairly promote people. He did not see that it might recruit potential leaders and winners who would make life better for everyone. I asked him if we could agree—as a starting point for our discussion—that I had been a pretty good basketball player. Yes, he said, we could agree on that. I asked him then, if he accepted that premise, to create a make-believe scenario where I was the same person, born to the same parents, possessing the same genetic, physical, and mental attributes, but by law and custom hadn't been allowed to play competitive basketball or even see a basketball game. All of a sudden, I said, I'm twenty-two and the Celtics call up and say, 'Listen, if you make the team, we want you to play for us.' Now I tell them that I've never even seen a basketball game, but they say, 'That's okay, this is affirmative action and we're going to train you, and if you're up to it, you'll be our twelfth man.' I then asked this student, should the Celtics have been able to do that or should they have had to fill up their roster with the twelve best available players? The twelve best players, he said. Okay, I answered, you're saying then that there should really be no opportunity for people who have not had professional training but whose skills may far surpass those who have had the training? He looked at me dumbfounded. The student was talking about equal opportunity as opposed to affirmative action, but my point then, and now, is that real opportunity is not possible until the system itself removes those artificial barriers that keep people from winning.

That student based his argument on something I believe: people do not have equal talents. The great majority do not possess the sorts of gifts that will be easily recognized, readily demanded, and amply rewarded. But how do all those with "ordinary" gifts still manage to win?

Let me start back at my old high school, McClymonds. Some years after I began playing with the Celtics, the mother of a student at the school contacted me. Her son, a six-foot-ten, left-handed basketball player, had heard my assembly talk as a freshman and was currently a graduating senior. He had tried, with the school's encouragement, to go on to the University of San Francisco but had been unable to get in. I met this student, liked him, and realized that he had, in a somewhat different way, been overlooked. He was not "the next Bill Russell," but was someone else entirely. What he wanted was a college education. I invited him to come back to Boston with me, and during that summer he went to a remedial English program and then got into Providence College, from which he graduated in four years. He was not a great basketball player, but just wanted the chance to use the abilities he had—and this he did. He understood the standards he had to deal with, he tried his best, and he created opportunity for himself.

This story points up the importance of creating opportunity and of finding ways to win no matter where you are.

> **Finding a way to win in life and business has little to do with your station in life. There are opportunities everywhere, and you must take advantage of them. I have memories of many who did just that.**

During my time with the Celtics, a guy named Frank Randall cleaned our locker room. Randy, as we called him was the first one there and the last to leave every night. If you ever saw the locker rooms in old Boston Garden, you'd know just how difficult his job was. The area we had was cramped, narrow, poorly lit, with no lockers, just hooks on the wall. When we got to the Garden for the game, Randy had our uniforms hanging on our hooks. He had taken the uniforms the night before and washed them at home. Red's office, the trainer's room, were just a couple of holes in the wall, stuck and jammed together.

If a player tossed something on the floor, a paper cup, an article of clothing, Randy's mild manner deserted him. "Don't be throwin' towels around, clean up after yerselves!" he'd bark out. It was important to him to have the place tip-top when we came in for work; he believed it helped us win games. Over the years, every player we had knew that he was as much a part of our team as anyone else. Celtic Pride was as real to him as to any of the rest of us.

Randy could have gone about business doing less, not more, having little or no concern for job standards, seeing little or nothing in his work that had opportunity in it. But in every respect, Randy epitomized my idea of how everyone can be a winner. Randy knew, absolutely, how a locker room could best be run. There was a real difference to him between just picking up, doing the laundry, and setting out the uniforms and the running of a locker room of a world championship team. He saw the latter, always. His standards were the highest possible. No one worked harder at his job than he did. You could not have left a towel lying around because he wouldn't let you. He saw in what he did an opportunity to make himself an integral part of a championship team. When he talked about the team, he, like the rest of us, always used the word *we*.

In the corporate world, countless stories parallel Randy's, but they are easy to miss for the obvious but deceptive symbols of power and wealth. Take Larry Fish, the president and CEO of Citizens Financial Group. This is a fast-growing and highly successful banking and financial organization in Boston that has increasingly seen its profit margins grow as it has expanded into the community. For Fish, the success of the company is all about winning, but his idea of winning is not so far from Randy's—or mine. "You have to want it," he says, "you have to work at it, and it's never an accident. You need to be there at coffee in the morning and also when the lights get turned off."

CFG prides itself on the way it has organized itself as a team where each member is responsible, accountable, and present for everyone else. Larry Fish's idea is that you don't win alone but with a good team. Good teams make good things happen, but, he stresses, good things are invariably about being able to respond to customers' needs, always being there in the moment to work out solutions to problems. "You've got to wake up every day and realize it's the customers who let you win," he stresses. The annual report of CFG actually publishes the number of dog biscuits and lollipops the company hands out at its teller windows.

The idea of leadership is fundamental to Fish. But by leadership he means being at the disposal of his team and his customers, always being ready to address problems on the ground, in the moment, as they arise. He stresses the power of listening and taking advice, but he emphasizes that leaders ought to step aside if they are not prepared to make hard decisions. Everything is about making the company responsive. That includes a real relationship with the community. "If the company does well and customers do well, but the community is doing poorly, it doesn't matter," Fish says. "We are only as strong as the weakest link."

Countless stories are about this singular effort to personally create conditions for success, wherever you are, whatever you are doing. The time to win is always the present moment; the attitude of a winner is constant no matter what.

Time for our review of the key Russell Rules on why everyone can find a way to win in life and business.

RUSSELL RULES

Rule One: Look for the opportunity to win in every situation. Know precisely what the lines and boundaries of your field are and learn the standards of success, no matter how insignificant they may seem. Keep at this until you really understand the difference between putting in hours and really doing a job.

Rule Two: No matter how often you have heard this before, you and you alone have to come to grips with any definition of success; it has to be yours, not someone else's. Doing your best at what seems like a lousy job is not a means of survival but of seeing the possibilities of winning. The most common stumbling block to success is when people, for one reason or another, tell themselves their best efforts will neither be needed nor recognized. Those who can give four dollars' worth of work for every three dollars of pay will be doing far more than earning points with their boss, they will be creating their own conditions for success. Such success need only be a standard of pride in oneself. It will be enough, and more than likely, it will ultimately be recognized by others.

Rule Three: Take the first step to winning today. Make sure that you start from where you happen to find yourself. Don't wait for that better job, that greater opportunity, the raise or promotion you have coming, the dream you still have in the back of your mind. Now is the time. There will never be a better time, there is only this moment, this very moment wherever you happen to be, where the opportunity to see yourself as powerful and accomplished is right there, with you— always has been and always will be. Use it. Begin winning now.

What I most want to emphasize is that what is called for here is not self-improvement, but applying what you already have. You don't need to be better than you are.

Take what you have and put it to use. Russell's Rule for the Rest of the Road is to understand that success is never a destination and always a journey.

MAKING CELTIC PRIDE WORK FOR YOU

CELTIC PRIDE IS A CULTURE. IT IS NOT ONLY A WAY YOU SEE yourself, it is a way you want others to see you. As I said in the introduction, Celtic Pride was the guts of how our organization, our coaches, and our team made decisions. It was created, nurtured, and developed for one goal . . . winning.

Celtic Pride is both a cognitive concept and a deeply emotional one. It was such a strong concept that it clearly had an effect on whom we played against. After Frank Ramsey, John Havlicek, and the Boston Garden fans, it became our second "sixth man."

Celtic Pride has aged well. It goes much deeper than just our teams from 1956 to 1969. In fact, it is totally independent of any specific year's team. It is a legacy. A passion. As I wrote earlier, I am far prouder of being captain of the Boston Celtics than anything else in my career.

Once a Celtic, always a Celtic. Once a Celtic fan, always a Celtic fan. Once you've embraced Celtic Pride, you'll never be the same. I once said, and I think it's worth repeating here,

"After I die, I cannot go to heaven. Because after leaving the Celtic locker room, anywhere else is a step down."

I hope that through this book Celtic Pride and the results it delivers will become part of your life. It is a metaphor for commitment, team ego, active listening, toughness and tenderness, craftsmanship, personal integrity, rebounding and resilience, imagination and collaborative decision-making. Almost fifty years after its creation, its mystique is still embraced in Boston, Massachusetts, New England, and by fans everywhere.

Celtic Pride is about relationships. Not only between each of us in the Celtic organization, but between the organization and the community. When I played, I always felt the Celtics were at the forefront of social consciousness. Since I've retired, I have noticed how every year the Celtic organization has gotten more and more involved in the community. The organization has demonstrated the power of Celtic Pride by its commitment to the community, and in response, whether the team is doing well or not, the community's leadership has been increasingly supportive of the Celtic culture.

In part, my intention in writing this book was to make Celtic Pride a less mystical and more accessible experience.

Now that you have read this book, the demystification of the Boston Celtics legacy will allow you to change your life and those around you. It's about winning, but winning for purposeful achievement.

I'd like to share a few closing thoughts with you.

As I wrote in the introduction, when I decided to write *Russell Rules*, I wanted to make sure that the mystique that has attached itself to the Celtics over the years had no place in this book, except maybe in the story of the parquet floor—that floor was mysterious! In fact, *Russell Rules* is an exposé. It blows away the myths of Celtic Pride and sheds sunlight on the eleven characteristics the team possessed that allowed it to achieve designation as the greatest team in American sports history. My express purpose in writing this book was to make sure others could see how to emulate the success we enjoyed. I knew then and I know now that every player on our team, our coach, owner, everyone else, was living a culture, following a plan, executing it, learning from it, revising it as it went along, always with the sense that we, as a team, knew exactly what we were doing.

Celtic Pride is what I have tried to spell out in practical terms in this book.

I must say a word about an obvious tension that exists between reading and doing. To state a rule, to elaborate a lesson, is one thing, but at the end some heavy lifting must be done, and those who want to bring Celtic Pride into their lives, their businesses, must make sure to do it. No one can ease the way for you.

> *It's hard work being a winner. If it weren't, everyone would be doing it.*

In May 1999, there was a tribute and re-retirement of my jersey for the benefit of the National Mentoring Partnership and the Massachusetts Mentoring Partnership. Because of my team orientation, getting this much public recognition and adulation made for an embarrassing night for me, but I had

agreed to participate because I felt it would provide an important platform for mentoring. Mentoring is important to the
future of America. The National Mentoring Partnership,
America's gateway to mentoring programs, was formed in 1991
to locate and create programs where those in business could
mentor younger people trying to find their way. According to a
recent study by the Partnership, there are 13.6 million at-risk
children in the United States. Currently only four hundred
thousand of them have anyone who could be considered a
mentor, guiding and steering them through their early lives.
Mentoring has always been part of my life. Whether with some
of yesterday's or today's players, young people whose lives have
crossed with mine, or others in the community whose rudder
has failed them . . . it's part of my consciousness. Interestingly
enough, researchers have studied young people with mentors
and those without them. According to these studies, young
people with mentors are less likely to do drugs, smoke, drink,
be absent from school, or engage in violent acts.

The implications of this study are enormous and signifi-
cant. To me it reinforces the belief in how possible it is for
young people, clearly economically disadvantaged, to become
part of a winning team. Mentoring is not hard work. Mentoring is about creating an awakening. It is breathing life into
abilities, capabilities, and potential that are living under the
surface but need to see the sunlight. Mentoring is as old as the
human race and is about redefining teamwork in a new context. It's a collaboration. Mentoring is the gift of a relationship.

As the months and days grew closer to the night of the Bill
Russell tribute, I uncharacteristically must have done more
than one hundred interviews to build awareness of mentoring

and the mentoring event. As I checked into the hotel in Boston, I was overwhelmed by the outpouring of attention and affection the evening was receiving. The night of the event, Wilt and I shared a car to the FleetCenter. I have always enjoyed police escorts. After having been on the receiving end of a few speeding tickets, I find a certain smile comes over me while speeding through the streets of Boston behind a police officer on a motorcycle instead of the other way around.

It was an intimate evening: twelve thousand Celtic fans in the FleetCenter with no game scheduled. One of my most favorite divas, Aretha Franklin, sang the national anthem, my friends Bill Cosby and Bryant Gumbel cohosted, and Tom Brokaw, Jim Brown, George Plimpton, Julius Erving, and Frank Deford offered humorous and moving reflections on our relationships. All my teammates were there, many of my opponents, my family, and great friends from all walks of life. The evening was one of the most emotional I've ever experienced and gave me an opportunity I had never taken before to tell all those fans whom I share Celtic pride with how much I have always loved them.

But during the tribute a few moments were particularly special.

Having thirty-two of the NBA's fifty great players there or on film was important to me. The honor from my peers was overwhelming and has always meant something very special. Their participation dramatized their respect and affection for me, and that was ultimately what meant the most.

Another memory I have was walking offstage at the end of the evening and seeing my father surrounded by my fans. I got nervous until I realized that "Mr. Charlie" was signing autographs. Can you imagine, a Russell giving autographs like that?

I have one last thought concerning the tribute. Throughout the evening, I thought it was supposed to be a celebration, but I had the feeling that I was reading my life off a long, tall tombstone. People adopt the strangest tones, use the most solemn words, when they talk about the past. My friend and former teammate John Thompson had it right when he said I would rather have eaten a bug than been there that night.

That night in Boston I had a few moments with so many folks, and it was a time to again let them know how special they each were. I used that time to let my teammates know, individually, in my own way, how much I had always cared for and respected them. Our bond deepened. We were young men when we quit playing, we are older men today—but we are closer now than we ever were.

Sometimes I see Cousy when I go to Boston. For years he has been a Celtic broadcaster. He can analyze a situation on the floor as quickly as anyone in the game, his eye is as sharp as it was when he ran a fast break.

Many of my teammates are successful men forty years later. Bill Sharman took his hard-nosed and disciplined game with him when he left Boston and made a brilliant career for himself, first as a coach then as an executive. He was the architect, along with Jerry West, of the great Los Angeles Laker teams of the eighties. Sharman devised methods of his own as a coach that have since been imitated by every coach in basketball. When a team, any team, has a game scheduled, they have a morning shoot-around. Bill is the guy who invented that, figuring out that if players got loose, went over game strategy earlier in the day, they would be more ready, physically and mentally, to compete that night. Anytime I was with him, I was always aware, without his ever having to say a word, how much Celtic Pride was an ongoing part of his life.

From the start, K.C. Jones was always enormously respectful of others. That made him a great competitor and teammate. He never minimized an opponent's (or teammate's) abilities or intelligence. He was always trying to learn from them. When he finished playing, he went into coaching, leading the Celtics to four divisional titles and two NBA Championships in five years.

Frank Ramsey was always one of my favorite teammates. He, like the rest of us, would really tense up before the play-offs and the championships. When he tensed up, he would develop a stutter. Frank would sit us down and say, "Na-na-now fellas, this is nh-nh-not the regular season anymore. Wa-wa-we're not playing fur Walter Brown's money, we're playing fur our money . . . na, na, no we're playing fur my money." This would just tear us up and help the team relax. With the salaries of the times some players could double their salary with the play-off money. Frank was always focusing on what was important. And that was also true in how he contributed when he played. He was more than just our sixth man. He could come into the game as either a guard or a forward and play as well as if he were a starter in either position. Frank was comfortable being Frank Ramsey.

At our year-end break-up celebration dinners Frank would have a few glasses of champagne and then invite me to come spend a few weeks during the summer in Kentucky with him. Well, in the sixties that wasn't going to happen. I would laugh and say to him, "Frank, I know you've had enough drinks to seriously invite me to spend a few weeks with you in Kentucky. But I have not had enough drinks to accept." We all started laughing.

Tom "Satch" Sanders, who is now an executive with the NBA, also provided us with so many laughs because he is such a funny guy. I have always loved the way he could tell a story. Since Satch had come from New York City and graduated from NYU, he had never needed to learn how to drive. When he got to the Celtics, he had never driven a car because he'd spent his life riding the subway. In Boston, he had to learn. So he started taking driving lessons. But because he was quite ner-vous about it, he'd practice at three in the morning when he thought no one else would be on the street. One night after a big snow he went out to practice in the middle of the night. Because many of the side streets weren't plowed, he had a little trouble that night. By his guesstimate he sideswiped four or five cars and had a rainbow of colors on the doors of his car. An-other time, actually on the day he got his license, he was driv-ing to practice when a fire truck came up behind him. He got nervous and kept slowing down to try to find a place to pull over, but snow kept him from finding an opening. He kept looking in the rearview mirror and the fire engine was just locked on his tail. Suddenly, he heard a bump. He looked ahead to see a police officer on his hood. The police officer climbed off the hood and came up to Tom's window with a real attitude. He demanded to see Tom's license. The officer took a look and said to Tom, "You've only had your license for one day." Tom said, "I know." The exasperated officer said, "Get out of here."

Nearly all my teammates understood Celtic Pride in terms of what needed to be done to make us winners. John Havlicek, who was our other great sixth man, told a reporter one time that starting wasn't as important as finishing. How to win meant doing exactly what was called for. John was completely devoid of pretension. He seemed so free of ego that it was hard in the beginning to coax him into shooting, so intent was he on getting the ball to everyone else, on making sure he ran plays and played defense correctly. Away from the court, the same thing. No pretension, no swagger, just doing whatever was called for. He used to hang his socks out to dry in the locker room. People constantly teased him about it. A reporter asked him one day why he did that. "My socks have to dry out" was the plain answer he gave.

I've continued to see Red over the years. He was eighty-three last year and is still as sharp and as engaging as ever—same as my father, who is even older. Red has changed his eyeglasses, but he is just as cranky and still smokes the same battery of foul-smelling cigars. He lives in Washington and remains quite active. He is still able to play a vigorous game of squash (one of his squash partners is Sam Jones's son), and he is still a keen observer of the game and the world around him. We still talk regularly. It goes something like this: "Red, how ya doing?" "I'm okay." "All right, bye." And when we are both in Boston for a Celtic event or game, we close out the evening the same way we did thirty and forty years ago by having dinner at his favorite Chinese restaurant.

At that National Mentoring Partnership tribute, Red came out onstage, chomping on one of his bombs, looked at me, winked, and then said to the twelve thousand fans who were hanging on his every word that he had a Bill Russell story to tell.

He related how at one point he had been unusually

disappointed with the way the team had been practicing. He had become worried. "Give me just twenty minutes of hard practice," he urged one day, "twenty minutes is all I'm asking." He said he didn't get it (I hadn't remembered that part of the story). The next day (which remains vivid in my mind), he related how he showed up with six cigars, which he laid out side by side on a table. "I'm prepared to sit here and smoke each one down until I get twenty consecutive minutes of hard practice," he said to us. He enjoyed telling how much the desire to avoid his cigar smoke spurred us on—especially me. After ten minutes, Red said, he blew his whistle, told us that was it for the day—and now thirty-five years later confessed that his cigar ploy had been the biggest mistake of his life. "Russell was killing his teammates, he gave me the greatest ten minutes of his career, and I had to call it off to save my team," he said. "I shoulda figured out how to lay out six cigars before every playoff game we had!" Actually, Red knew I was never a practice player, and he never badgered me over the years to change my ways, because he always got from me what he and I both wanted—winning championships.

What makes my teammates, coach, and I so close is that the experience of being a successful team has never left us. Who we are today has nothing to do with reliving our glory years but everything to do with the mutual understanding we continue to share about how winning takes place. Celtic Pride isn't a diploma, it's how to manage your life. The principles that guided us then are just as relevant today.

I am often asked about today's NBA players and teams. The assumption is that Celtic Pride is a thing of the past. It is not. Begin with the question of money. Players today can make more in a single year than the budgets of some small nations.

We are often told that that ruins players. I don't believe it. No amount of money could have slowed Michael Jordan or cut into his determination to make his team a champion. I see players like Kevin Garnett and I am reminded all over again of the joy and pleasure of playing. This is completely independent of money. For me, there isn't enough money on the planet to induce me to wish I were playing today, and for players really into the game, the absence of money, in the end, would not matter. In the present as in the past, the game is about winning.

While the game today remains much the same as the one I left, there are some important differences in the level of competition. With expansion, to be competitive, the coaches have had to rely more on fundamentals—defensive setups especially. Most of the draft picks are selected because of their offensive statistics. If you're a team playing the Lakers, for example, how do you compete if you've lost more road games than you've won? You have to come up with defensive schemes to offset the talent. But the fundamentals are still the same as when I played.

Expansion has diminished the depth chart of most teams. That's a problem. For example, in my fourth year in the league, I had four guards: Bob Cousy, Bill Sharman, K.C. Jones, and Sam Jones. All of them are in the Hall of Fame. Expansion, not to mention money, would make it extremely unlikely for a current team to have that kind of talent at its disposal. But any team that has a solid nucleus and manages to hold its roster together long enough can put a winner on the floor today if they approach the game with the same principles we used.

So how can Celtic Pride work for you? What can you do in

a practical way to implement the lessons and rules contained in this book? Let's briefly review our lessons:

1. Curiosity is a key to commitment and, specifically, to problem solving. Curiosity will always allow you to ask the right questions . . . Why? What if? How?

2. Everything you do begins with yourself, but for you to use ego to win, you have to make it all about your team. Winning is a team sport and can only be accomplished through team ego.

3. Listening lets you hear what isn't being said as much as what is. Active listening helps you find a new language that helps others listen more effectively.

4. Toughness and tenderness are not opposites but partners in effective leadership.

5. Invisibility is learning how to make your opponents believe they can't beat you even when you're not there.

6. Craftsmanship is to you what quality is to your product or service. It involves making yourself the most complete colleague, leader, or parent you can be.

7. Personal integrity is about setting standards and your choices, responsibilities, and commitments.

8. Rebounding is changing the flow of the game from defense to offense. From reaction to action. It is about developing the highest level of resilience.

9. Imagination is the gateway to innovation. Innovation is the foundation of differentiation. Winning is the greatest form of differentiation.

10. Decision-making is for leaders. Decision-making is most effective when it is inclusionary, not exclusionary.

11. Everyone has an opportunity to win in life. Winning is hard work. Winning is a team sport. It is the culmination of attitude, aptitude, and appetite.

The National Mentoring Partnership tribute was capped off by an event that is perhaps the most effective metaphor to close this book. It was at the public re-retiring of my number and the hoisting of it to the rafters of the arena.

That was not something I looked forward to. As I wrote in lesson two, when my number was originally retired in the 1970s, I wanted no part of a public ceremony. I let the Celtics know. Red was appalled. I couldn't back out, I had to be there when my number went up, he said. No, I said, no public ceremonies for me. If you want to honor someone, do it in a way that is important to them. We went back and forth over this, and then one day when I was due in Boston to do a broadcast, Red confidently informed me that my number was going to be retired at the Garden that night. He had me cornered—he thought. But I told him I still wouldn't do it. What about the broadcast, he wanted to know, was I also going to skip out on that? What I was willing to do, I told him, was to have the ceremony with only my teammates present. So that night, an hour before the Garden opened, Red and the Celtic players still on the team from the time I'd played stood in the middle of the floor and raised my number before eighteen thousand empty seats.

My reasoning then (and now) was that I played for my team. It was a basic principle that I felt I couldn't violate without giving up an important piece of myself. At the National Mentoring Partnership event, the re-retirement ceremony was a little different. The banner that was raised to the roof did not just have my number on it. It was a single banner, silky white and green, but it contained all of the other retired numbers of my Boston Celtic teammates. Red and I stood together in a darkened FleetCenter, on the fabled parquet floor, which they transplanted from the old Boston Garden, spotlights bearing down on us, and we each took hold of the long rope together, winked at each other, and hand over hand hoisted the banner of our team, the symbol of my personal success, to the rafters.

It was the banner of Celtic Pride.

ACKNOWLEDGMENTS

I would like to thank Alan Hilburg for his tireless efforts on my behalf as an adviser, business partner, and counselor. He is the architect of my renaissance and my friend. I also would like to thank Laurie (Alan's remarkable wife) and their children, Carolyn, Natalie, and my godson, Ben, for standing beside Alan during the creation and development of this book.

ABOUT THE AUTHORS

Bill Russell is a true original, an innovator, and he defines winning. He won eleven NBA Championships in thirteen seasons with the Boston Celtics and coached the team to two of those championships. He was the first African American to coach a professional sports team and the first and only player/coach to win two NBA Championships without an assistant. He was the first athlete to win an NCAA Championship, an Olympic Gold Medal, and an NBA Championship all in one year. He was named the Twentieth Century's Greatest Team Player by *Sports Illustrated*, and HBO recognized Russell as "The Greatest Winner of the Twentieth Century." He lives with his family in Seattle, Washington.

David Falkner is the author of several highly acclaimed books on sports including *Sadaharu Oh: A Zen Way of Baseball*, *The Last Yankee*, and *Great Time Coming: The Life of Jackie Robinson from Baseball to Birmingham*.